# GOLF'S FORGOTTEN HERO

# THE LIFE of JOHN MCDERMOTT

Kevin Kenny

GOLF'S FORGOTTEN HERO THE LIFE of JOHN MCDERMOTT
by Kevin Kenny

Lettertec Publishing
Springhill House,
Carrigtwohill
Co. Cork
Republic of Ireland
www.selfpublishbooks.ie

For my friend,

PGA Hall of Fame member, Marty Kavanaugh,

who encouraged me to honor the life and career

of John McDermott.

# Acknowledgments

There are many people to whom I am deeply indebted in regard to the publication of this book. In terms of my research, the team at the USGA Library in Far Hills, New Jersey, was particularly helpful. I am thinking here of Mike Trostel who wrote the foreword for the book. But also, Hilary Coe-Cronheim, Victoria Nenno, Maggie Lagle, and in particular Tara Valente who has been so enthusiastic and helpful throughout the process. I am very grateful to Merion G.C. in John MacDermott's home city of Philadelphia, for providing me with so much archive material. In this regard, my thanks to Paula Kelly, John Capers, and especially Wayne Morrison. I am also grateful to Michelle Dooley from the St Francis de Sales parish for providing me with material on John McDermott's early days. Many thanks also to Nancy Sullivan from the Historical Society of Montgomery County. As always, my thanks to Marty Kavanaugh for his advice and support. And similar thanks goes to Paul Cervantes. My gratitude also to the Aronimink club for some invaluable material, in particular, John Cunningham and David Penske. And finally, thanks to my wife Celia for her help with the editing process.

# FOREWORD

*By Michael Trostel*

If you asked one hundred sports historians who America's first golf hero was, chances are you would hear names ranging from Francis Ouimet and Walter Hagen to Gene Sarazen and Bob Jones.

Admittedly, it is a subjective question as many players from the early 20th century have the resume to lay claim to that title. We have display cases dedicated to all four of the players mentioned above in the USGA Golf Museum. So, while you would be hard pressed to identify a definitive answer, there is one player who I would argue should be a part of that conversation that likely isn't: John J. McDermott.

I didn't know much about McDermott when I started at the USGA in 2006. I grew up in Massachusetts and had often heard about the legend of Ouimet, who incredibly won the 1913 U.S. Open at The Country Club in Brookline as a 20-year-old amateur who lived across the street. But as I started to dig deeper, I realized Ouimet wasn't the first American to win his national championship, nor the youngest.

Perhaps Hagen summed it up best when he said that McDermott was the golfer who "opened the gates to American homebreds." International players had dominated the U.S. Open since its inception in 1895; the first 16 championships were all won by players born in Scotland or England.

In the 1910 U.S. Open, McDermott came closer to winning than any American had to that point. He led the championship after 54 holes before losing to Alex Smith in an 18-hole playoff, that also included Alex's brother Macdonald.

The following year, McDermott once again found himself in a three-way playoff, but this time finished the job, defeating Mike Brady and George Simpson to earn the trophy. At 19 years, 10 months, and 11 days, he remains the only teenager to have claimed the title.

The Philadelphia native won again in 1912, becoming just the second player to successfully defend his title. His 72-hole total of 294 on a par 74 course also made him the first player to break par in the championship.

Journalist Grantland Rice wrote, "John was the greatest golfer America has ever produced, amateur or professional, when it came to a combination of nerve, coolness and all-around skill from the tee to the green."

McDermott seemed poised for decades of sustained success, but in 1914 he was a passenger aboard a ship that collided with another vessel during a transatlantic journey. Following that traumatic experience, McDermott was never the same. Over the following decades, he suffered from mental illness and competed in golf tournaments only sporadically.

It was a jarring rise-and-fall, one that seemed more likely to occur in a Shakespearian tragedy. But more than a century after he reached golf's pinnacle, McDermott's story is still highly relevant.

His struggles with mental health are some of the first documented in sports. Today, thousands of athletes at all levels of sports continue to fight courageously against the pressures heaped on them by society, the media and themselves. They strive to overcome traumatic events in their lives that have inhibited their abilities find joy and fulfilment in competition.

McDermott's career was cut short, but his impact on the game has been long-lasting. His accomplishments helped to grow golf during its earliest years in the United States and need to be recognized as seminal in the game's development and popularization in America.

*Michael Trostel is Historian with the United States Golf Association (USGA) in Far Hills, New Jersey.*

# Contents

# Preface

I have already written biographies of two players who have graced the game of golf. One of these was Patty Berg, whose tournament record, added to her longevity, placed her at the top table in the history of women's golf in America, and beyond. In contrast, another book, was on the life of Ralph Guldahl who, for a few glorious years, in the late 1930's, was arguably the best player in the world, never mind the United States. Journalists often used the term "shooting star" to describe his rapid rise and fall from the top of the game. However, there is another player in the history of American golf whose rise and decline outdid that of Guldahl, and in the most tragic of circumstances. His name was John McDermott and if ever a top golfer deserved the word "comet" attached to his name, it was this Irish/American son of Philadelphia.

John J. McDermott came into the world of professional golf while still in his teens and at a time when British-born professionals ruled the game both in Britain and in the United States. The period was the first decade of the 20th century and commentators in America feared that, while golf was growing in popularity across the land, there was no American-born professional equipped to take on the mostly Scottish-bred professionals, who ruled the game both in terms of securing the plum club positions, and regarding competitive success, notably in the U.S. Open Championship. John McDermott changed this within the space of three years. In 1910, at the age of 19, he tied for first place in the National Open, losing the play-off to Scottish-born Alex Smith. And then, in both 1911 and 1912, he won the U.S. Open title, thus becoming the first American-born golfer to triumph in this, the greatest of all American golf championships.

However, within a few years, he had virtually retired from golf and was to spend the rest of his days in a mental institution. And, while there have been many "What Happened to John McDermott" articles, to-date, we have not seen a more complete account of his life. I hope that this book will fill in some of the gaps that exist regarding our knowledge of John McDermott, his career, and his life.

# Introduction

The dean of modern American golf writers, Herbert Warren Wind, was not born when Francis Ouimet created history by beating Harry Vardon and Ted Ray to win the 1913 U.S. Open at the Country Club, Brookline. But as his career developed, he demonstrated, perhaps better than anyone, the importance of what took place. He described Ouimet's victory as "The Shots Heard Round the World" and the reference to the opening skirmishes of the American Revolution in 1775, conveyed the magnitude of Ouimet's victory. Wind, who was not given to sycophancy, went on to say that "the luckiest thing, however, that happened to American golf was that its first great hero was Francis Ouimet."[1] And that, "The hundreds of thousands of Americans who had been inspired by Francis Ouimet's victory to take up golf found that their hero was an even greater person than most heroes: he was a fine man."[2] Ouimet's place in American golf history has never been questioned and rightly so. As a caddie, this young amateur defeated two of the game's giants in Vardon and Ray. Ouimet also brought what was often considered an elite sport to a much wider audience, and he began American golf's long hegemony. He was undoubtedly the United States first golfing superstar whose face, in time, would feature on a postage stamp.

A far lesser- known figure in the history of American golf is John McDermott and yet, but for a series of unfortunate circumstances, he might have beaten Ouimet to the honor of first American golf hero. Like Ouimet, McDermott too came from a modest background and he also graduated through the caddie ranks. Then, in 1911, he became the first home-born professional to win the U.S. Open title. McDermott then repeated the feat a year later. To place this into context, before McDermott's successes *all* National Open winners were either British born or were imported professionals from across the Atlantic who had made their home in the United States. Perhaps the summit of British supremacy in America was 1900 when Harry Vardon toured the United States to promote Spalding's Vardon Flyer guttie ball. As Wind again recalled, "In a long series of exhibition matches, Vardon

1 H. W. Wind, *The Story Of American Golf* (New York: Alfred A.Knopf, 1975) p 85

2 *Ibid*

played against our best homebreds and the outstanding Anglo-American pros, and dropped only one match. He took time off to compete in the U.S. Open and finished nine strokes ahead of the field."[3]

So, if it was not the great Vardon "taking time off" a tour to win the U.S. Open, it was the imports who dominated that national championship and it is in this context that John McDermott's first success, as a raw nineteen- year- old, should be seen. This was truly the stuff of a boy hero. Instead, John McDermott was often reduced to a footnote in the glittering history of American golf. Against such a background, this book will seek to explore the reasons for this sharp rise and tragic decline. It will chart his life from a modest home in West Philadelphia, to the caddy yard at Aronimink and later to the professional's position at Atlantic City Country Club. It will look in detail at his two National Open successes, his attempts to win The Open Championship, and then to his mental breakdown and his institutionalization. In this regard, this book aims to offer some possible explanations as to the reasons for John McDermott's mental health issues. The author hopes that this account will provide at least some insights into one of the most important stories in American golf history: that of the nation's first golfing star.

3 Ibid, p. 41

# Chapter One
# EARLY DAYS

For much of the first half of the twentieth century, Grantland Rice was recognized as America's finest and most influential sportswriter. And while, among other sports, he covered football and baseball, his contribution to golf was arguably his greatest legacy. His friendship with, and writings on Bobby Jones, added to his influence in developing what became golf's "Fourth Major," The Masters, are testimony to this. So, Rice's words deserve to be treated with respect, both then and now. In 1916 he wrote that the "passing" of John McDermott was of great significance as the American player was "the sole barrier between the homebreds and the outside enemies."[4]

The word "passing" here was used metaphorically as McDermott was still only 25 years old. Rather it referred to the remarkable decline in the form of this two-time U.S. Open Champion who, in 1911, became the first home grown American to win the U.S. Open and retain it a year later. In doing so, McDermott had shown Americans and the world that a native-born professional could beat both the twin forces of the top amateurs and the foreign pros, the "outside enemies" to which Rice referred. Writing in 1916, Rice paid this tribute to the two-time U.S. Open champion. "To our off-side way of thinking, John McDermott was the greatest golfer America has produced, amateur or professional when it comes to a combination of nerve, coolness and all around skill from the tee to the cup. McDermott had no weakness in any part of his game, and what is more to the point, he was pretty sure to be of his best under the heaviest fire."[5] And, Rice finished his piece by claiming that, "There isn't any question but that McDermott would have been to American golf what Vardon is to British play if John J. had not been forced out through fate just at the moment when he was comping upon the uplands of his career."[6]

---

4 *The Montgomery Advertiser*, October 23, 1916)
5 *Ibid*
6 *Ibid*

There is a certain poignancy in the fact that as early in the life of John McDermott as 1916, Rice was writing in the past tense, but sadly this proved to be correct. Later, Herbert Warren Wind, who would take over from Grantland Rice as America's pre-eminent golf writer, made the following comments about McDermott's decline. "For two or three seasons, while his nerve held high, the 130 pound bantam cock was almost as good as he thought he was................. And then, almost as quickly as he appeared, McDermott vanished. The nerves on which he had relied on so heavily to carry him to the top suddenly stopped." Wind then finished his comments on a poignant note, "Four scant years after Johnny McDermott had won at Chicago, golfers had to pause a moment and ponder before they could remember the name of the little firecracker who was the first American to win the United States Open."[7] The question of John McDermott's "passing" into decline is one of the great mysteries in American golf history because, for a three-year period from 1910 to 1912, he dominated the U.S. Open.

In Gaelic Irish, the name McDermott means son of Diarmaid and more literally it means "free from envy" or "free man." Whatever about being free from envy, all the evidence suggests that John McDermott sought to become his own man- a free man indeed. In this regard, as his life and career progressed, McDermott certainly became his own man in that he felt free from the opinions of others, and his various eccentricities marked him out as different to his peers. McDermott certainly lived up to the literal meaning of his Gaelic name.

John McDermott was born on August 12 1891. The family home was located at 1234 South 50th St, in an Irish suburb of West Philadelphia. McDermott's father, John Sr, was of Irish stock, one of many in the city who claimed such ancestry. Even before the influx of Irish immigrants in the post-Famine era, Philadelphia was home to many Irish families who had settled in the city since the 18th century. Indeed, it was estimated that by 1850, 17.6 per cent of Philadelphia's population was Irish. And while the Irish undoubtedly made a mark in the city, their arrival was not without its problems. Donald MacRaild recorded that "American Puritanism gave the Irish considerable grounds to feel isolated, excluded, outcast and below." And in reference to the sporadic Orange/Catholic riots, Philadelphia was dubbed the "city of brotherly hate."[8]

---

7 Wind, p 68.

8 D.M. MacRaild, *The Great Famine And Beyond* (Dublin: Irish Academic Press, 2000), p 52.

As in many other American cities, the immigrants found work through manual labor that was much in demand. In the case of John McDermott Sr, it was delivering mail that provided a living for his family which consisted of his wife Margaret, (nee Smith) John Jr and sisters Gertrude and Alice. The Catholic Church also flourished in late 19th century Philadelphia as it accommodated the influx of Irish migrants. And one parish near the McDermott home, St Francis de Sales, was to figure prominently in McDermott's life. His mother, Margaret, was a choir member there and it was where John Jr was confirmed on May 29, 1902. It was also recorded that his father, John Sr, donated $8 to the parish relief debt in 1894.[9] Throughout his days, John McDermott's Catholic faith was an integral part of his life.

In the early days of professional golf in America, the caddy yard featured prominently as a breeding ground for aspiring players and John McDermott was no different. As fortune would have it, his maternal grandfather owned a home that was located next to the Belmont Golf Association nine-hole course. There was an old barn on the Belmont course that, according to legend, was the home of the Native American Chief, Aronimink. The name Aronimink was quickly adopted by the members and when, in 1926, the club eventually settled in the Donald Ross designed course at Newtown Square, it became one of America's elite clubs. Over the years Aronimink has hosted majors such as the U.S. PGA and U.S. Amateur Championships. When visiting his grandfather, the young McDermott quickly discovered this new "playground" and well before his teenage years, he had developed a gift for caddying. From then on, golf took over his life and as well as caddying, he and his friend, Morrie Talman, began playing the game in a stretch of orchard land close to Aronimink's seventh hole. Morrie Talman would later serve as head pro at Whitemarsh Valley for 40 years.

Even at this stage, however, certain traits were in evidence in McDermott's personality that would stay with him throughout his career. As Rhonda Glenn recorded, "Even as a youngster McDermott had a difficult personality. A small guy, he was brash and other caddies called him a bully.'"[10] Notwithstanding McDermott's somewhat awkward disposition, Aronimink's head professional, Walter Reynold's, was impressed by the youngster's earnestness and love of golf and he gave him some lessons as well as teaching him the rudiments of club making. Similarly,

9 Francis De Sales archives

10 R. Glenn, *Museum Moment: When the Cheering Stopped: The Tragedy of John J. McDermott*, (New Jersey: The USGA Museum) January 6, 2011.

when Bill Byrne took over as head pro at Aronimink, he too passed on some of his knowledge to McDermott. Coincidentally, Byrne was also of Irish stock having been born in England to Irish parents. Perhaps their shared ancestry helped form a bond between the two men as in later years, McDermott was quick to acknowledge the help he received from Byrne.

In 1906, as was the norm for young men from working class homes, the 15 -year- old McDermott was told by his father to leave school and find a trade of some description. Typically, this would have meant going to work in a factory. McDermott, however, saw only golf as his future and became the assistant professional at the Camden Country Club, New Jersey. McDermott was also assistant pro at Merion for a period between 1908 and 1910. Merion would later figure prominently in the life of John McDermott. And, for a short time, he held a similar position at the Merchantville Club in New Jersey where, despite his at times difficult personality, it was recorded that "He had good manners, didn't drink or smoke and seldom missed Sunday Mass."[11] These qualities added to his emerging talent for the game, in time persuaded the Atlantic City Country Club, New Jersey, to offer him the professional's job. This period at the Atlantic Club would prove pivotal in John McDermott's development into a top golfer.

In the history of 20th century professional golf, it is generally accepted that nobody out- worked Ben Hogan. His words, "the secret is in the dirt" became a mantra for many players such as Gary Player, who came close to matching Hogan for hours spent on the practice ground. However, more than 20 years before Hogan first went on tour, the young John McDermott had already worked out that if he wanted to become a champion, practice was the only way. At quiet Merchantville, there was plenty of time to work on his game but it was at Atlantic City that his appetite for practice became widely known. His sister Alice recalled that John McDermott lived close to the club and that "He would be on the practice field as soon as it was light, about 5am, and hit balls until 8am when he would then operate the pro shop. After his day's teaching, he would go out and play. Often, he told us, he finished in twilight with somebody holding a lantern."[12] It was said that part of his practice routing involved McDermott laying out a newspaper as a target for his mid-irons with which he became especially proficient.

---

11 Glenn

12 Glenn

Physically, at five foot seven, McDermott was not tall but as we have seen from the careers of Ben Hogan and Gary Player, height is not a necessity for a champion golfer. What McDermott did possess, however, was a pair of strong hands and arms and these enabled him to achieve great power. McDermott's swing was seen as quite free and even loose, with a pronounced pivot and he also used an open stance. What distinguished McDermott, however, was his grip.

A perfect view of John McDermott's unusual double overlapping grip (courtesy Merion Golf Club).

At this time, the Vardon overlapping grip was taking over from the more traditional two-handed grip popularized by the early Scottish professionals. McDermott did overlap, but with two fingers instead of the usual one. Former U.S. Open Champion, Jim Furyk used the double overlapping grip, and from an earlier era, Ireland's Harry Bradshaw did likewise. Bradshaw was a multi-tournament winner in the UK and Ireland and a successful Ryder Cup player. Bradshaw also tied Bobby Locke for the 1949 Open Championship. Even if McDermott had received advice from both Walter Reynolds and Bill Byrne, all the evidence suggests that it was the hours spent on the practice ground where he found a method of hitting a golf ball that would stand up to the pressure of championship golf.

McDermott's entry into competitive golf began in earnest in 1907, when he shot the best score of 85 in the All-City Caddie Championship at Aronimink. Local knowledge was undoubtedly a factor here. Regarding tournament golf, his introduction was inauspicious. He played in the 1908 Philadelphia Championship but lost in the elimination round to Bill Byrne by 4/3. The following year, The U.S. Open was held at the Englewood Club in New Jersey, and the winner was England's George Sargent who continued the line of non-American-born players winning the U.S. Open title. His winning total of 290 was a Championship record. McDermott shot 322 and finished in 49th place. However, his confidence was in no way dented and, on his trip, McDermott placed an advertisement in a local New York newspaper challenging "any pro" to a $500 match over two rounds, with each player having home advantage for 18 holes. Playing golf with his own money would become a feature of McDermott's career. Typically, the winner of the National Open at that time received $300, so this was no small challenge. The only taker was Jimmy Campbell from Whitemarsh Valley who was beaten so badly in the first 18 at home, that he declined to play the second round. So, John McDermott returned home with some cash in his pocket, ***and*** the experience of playing in the U.S. Open. That experience would stand to him the following year when, while he was still at Merchantville, he made his first real impact on the world of golf in June 1910.

# Chapter Two
# 1910 THE PHILADELPHIA CRICKET CLUB

The U.S. Open of 1910 was held at the Philadelphia Cricket Club. The club, founded in 1854 and the oldest in American golf history, owed its name to a group of English students who wished to continue playing the game of cricket in their new home. Of the three courses that the club eventually housed, the 1910 Championship was held on the St Martins Course that was originally a nine-hole lay-out but which in 1897 graduated to 18 holes. The course derived its name from the local Episcopal Church, St Martin in the Fields. The club, like many others of the day, was highly conservative and it was noted after the event, that "the Philadelphia Cricket Club gave the professionals the privileges of amateur players." And it was further noted that the members helped out by acting as scorers and that, "This scoring business is one of the disagreeable features of medal play golf."[13] Both comments very much reflected the golfing mores of the day in that the privileged amateur golfer was seen as being superior to his professional counterpart, and that the format predominantly played by the amateur, was a more desirable form of golf. But it was still medal play at the Cricket Club.

At this stage of his career, the 18 -year- old John McDermott was professional at the Merchantville Club in New Jersey and the 1910 Championship saw him return to his home town of Philadelphia. Not that many people noticed this confident youngster, for as U.S. Open historian, Robert Sommers, recorded," When he teed off in the first round hardly anyone was aware that Johnny McDermott was in the field."[14] There was good reason for this. The U.S. Open was first held in 1895 at Newport Rhode Island. That year and up to 1898, it was played over 36 holes, and the first winner was Englishman, Horace Rawlings. This trend was to continue with

13 *The Golfers Magazine*, July 1910.
14 *The Junior Golfer*, 1911.

the National title being won only by British golfers. The homebreds were hardly seen as newsworthy, especially a little-known 18 -year- old with no track record. In 1910, the defending champion was Englishman George Sargent.

As with the British title, the U.S. Open at that time was played over two days and after round one, the leader was Tom Anderson Jr with a one under round of 72. Among those on 73 was Tom McNamara who would figure prominently in the career of John McDermott as a friend, rival, mentor, and as an exhibition partner. McNamara was very much of Boston/Irish stock and had strong family connections to the famed Lahinch Links on Ireland's south west coast. His cousin, Willie McNamara, was the club's first professional. The young Tom, like Francis Ouimet, learned the game by caddying at the Country Club, Brookline, where his brother Dan, was the caddy master. Later at Brookline, he came under the tutelage of club professional Willie Campbell who helped with his development. McNamara came very close the previous year when he lost a three- shot lead on the final nine before finishing runner-up to the eventual winner of the Championship, George Sargent. This was one of three second place finishes McNamara would have in the National Open. He would also have seven tour victories including the prestigious North and South and Western Opens.

McNamara was also influential in advising Rodman Wannamaker and others, on the formation of the PGA in 1916. In later years, he would become director of Wilson's golf division and was responsible for recruiting Gene Sarazen to the ranks of the equipment giant. His contribution to American golf was significant. Going into 1910, he could certainly claim to be the top home- born American professional and in the previous year's he achieved the honor of being the first home-bred professional to break 70 in the U..S. Open when he shot 69 at Englewood. Interestingly, in the month prior to the Championship McNamara prophetically said, "From my observations throughout the country, I am one of those who believe that it will not be many years before America will lead the world of golf."[15] Time would prove McNamara to be right. In that first round, John McDermott was in a group on 74 that included MacDonald Smith. And that afternoon, McDermott shot another 74 and finished the day on 148 only two shots back of leader Alex Smith.

15 *The Boston Herald*, May 22, 1910.

McDermott's great rival, Alex Smith is on the left with McDermott on the extreme right (courtesy Merion Golf Club).

Alex Smith was part of a Scottish golfing dynasty that was highly prominent in the early days of American professional golf. Hailing from Carnoustie on Scotland's east coast, in time the entire Smith family would emigrate and find a better life in America. But in the world of golf, it was the three brothers, Alex, Willie and MacDonald who would make their mark. At this stage, amongst other titles, Alex had won the U.S. Open in 1905 following his brother, Willie, who won the championship in 1899. And while the youngest brother, MacDonald never won a major championship, he too would have an outstanding career.

On the final morning, Alex Smith had a dreadful front nine of 43 and while he recovered to eventually card a 79, he was overtaken my McDermott's 75. The 18- year- old was now in prime position as he led by one from McNamara and two from Alex Smith. It looked as if America might have its first home-bred winner of the National Open. However, just as quickly as McDermott had taken the lead, the opening nine of the final round saw him surrender it. First, the younger of the Smith brothers shot an outstanding 33 while his brother, Alex, took 35. McDermott's 38 saw him trail the Scottish pair by one. In the end, it came down to the 240 yar 18th hole with McDermott trailing by one. Again, Robert Somers lyrically described the scene.

Despite McDermott's heroic finish, he needed some help to make the play-off. This came when Alex Smith, having driven the 18th green, three putted from

20 feet. McDermott's reaching the play-off may have been a surprise to the golfing world but there were reports that it was even more so to his family who, apparently, were unaware of his presence at the Cricket Club.[16]

The Championship finished on Saturday evening but the play-off did not take place until the following Monday. This was due to Philadelphia's "Blue Laws" that decreed that the Sabbath be reserved for prayer and that sporting activities should not take place. For the play-off it was reported that "The largest gallery which Philadelphia has ever known followed the men on Monday and were well repaid."[17] McDermott's opponents, the Smith brothers from Carnoustie, were formidable, even if the younger Smith's best days were yet to come. And, in an example of commercialism in golf in the early 20th century, sporting giant Spalding ran an advertisement headed "Triple Tie for Spalding Golf Balls," as all three contestants played that brand. The day of the play-off saw warm and dry weather and on a sartorial note, it was recorded that "The Smiths played in flannel trousers and outing shirts, but McDermott, despite excessive heat, remained faithful to his khaki coat over trousers and silk shirt."[18] However, it was not suggested that McDermott's more formal attire played any part in the outcome.

That McDermott was relatively unheard of was unquestionable, but on the morning of the play-off, there were indications that this was changing. *The Morning Post* declared that,

> Whether or not he wins the final test to-day, John McDermott of the Merchantville Field Club golf links is a hero in golf circles and has made his name known from coast to coast. The whole country has been watching the championship golf contests in Philadelphia but nobody ever heard of John McDermott before: that is not in the way they had heard of other big golfers who entered the race..........They found he was a youngster who a season ago had been a caddie.[19]

The brief but glorious era of the homebred caddy who rose to golf's summit had begun, and it had started to capture the imagination of the American public.

---

16 *Golf Digest*, June 1997.
17 *The American Golfer*, July 1910.
18 *The Evening Star*, June 21, 1910.
19 *The Morning Post*, June 20, 1910.

McDermott's swing was full and with a pronounced pivot (courtesy Merion Golf Club)

In the play-off it was Alex Smith who made the best start and McDermott trailed him by four after seven holes. The younger Smith was by now, struggling. However, McDermott fought back as he always did and a birdie three at the eight and a two at the short ninth saw the deficit cut to one at the end of the outward half: 37 for Alex Smith and 38 for McDermott. McDonald Smith was out in 41. Essentially the title was decided between the 11th and 14th holes when Smith's birdie-par-par-par run saw him gain three shots on McDermott and his final nine of 34 led to a score of 71. This excellent round was four ahead of McDermott's one-under 75, and six clear of his younger brother who recovered somewhat to shoot 77. It was the first of many disappointments MacDonald Smith would have in the majors. Reports indicate that it was McDermott's putting that let him down in the play-off, but his mid-iron play, that would be his signature shots during his career, drew widespread praise. This compliment was affirmed by renowned golf course architect and journalist, A.W. Tillinghast who later reported on his ability to achieve backspin with the mashie, "It was the real wrist shot." He said, "Like a man flicking a fly from his horse's back." According to Tillinghast, this wrist action added to his "supreme confidence is the secret of his astonishing play."[20] The purity of his strike was already a feature of McDermott's game and achieving bite or backspin with hickory shafts on fast greens was testimony to this.

---

20 W. Fields, *ESPN*, June 17, 2004.

However, if McDermott received praise for his golf, he did not leave the Philadelphia Cricket Club quietly. McDermott's fellow Irish-American, Tom McNamara, had attempted to become a mentor to the young pro but as A.W. Tillinghast recalled," even his fathering could not keep him on the leash during the week of practice previous to the championship and certainly Johnny was no shrinking violet."[21] What is true is that McDermott challenged all comers to a match for "real money" and Tillinghast also recalled that he addressed Alex Smith as "Schmidty" and challenged him to play for "dough."[22] For a rookie to speak to a senior pro such as Alex Smith like this was seen as tantamount to an insult. You had to earn your stripes before you could play practice rounds with members of the golfing elite, never mind aggressively challenge them to play for "dough." Certainly, Alex Smith took exception to his behavior and dismissed the youngster, telling him to, "run along and not bother him."[23] But characteristically, McDermott did not forget this slight and after the play-off it was recorded that "The insult from days before roiled inside him......Smith having no sense of the situation walked over and said, 'hard luck kid' to which McDermott responded, "I'll get you next year you big tramp."[24] McDermott may have got away with "I'll get you next year" which could have been regarded as "fighting talk" from a raw professional. The "big tramp" reference, however, said to an experienced and respected pro, was seen as a step too far. He may have been standing up for himself, but such outbursts would feature again in McDermott's career and bring him a great deal of unwanted attention.

And it seemed as if the feud between Alex Smith and John McDermott endured. When Alex Smith died in 1930, his obituary made reference to McDermott. As was well known, from early on and throughout his career, John McDermott's signature shot was the mashie (or medium iron). Smith would have none of this and apparently used to "scoff at the idea" that the man "who gained a reputation for uncanny skill with the mashie, equalled or surpassed, either Gil or Mac."[25] The Gil referred to Englishman Gilbert Nicholls and "Mac" his fellow Scotsman, and younger brother, MacDonald Smith. Perhaps, this was purely a professional opinion but it could also be seen as the inventors of the game and those who brought the game to America, continuing to pass judgement on the homebreds.

---

21 A.W. Tillinghast, *Reminiscences Of The Links,* (Tree Wolf Productions, 1998), p 94/95.

22 *Ibid.*

23 *Ibid.*

24 S. Eubanks, *Global Golf Post*, June 7, 2018.

25 *The Brooklyn Daily Eagle*, May 11, 1930.

However, there was also a happier outcome to John McDermott's experience in Philadelphia. In the early decades of the 20th century (and for many years after) one of the rewards for a strong tournament performance was the possibility of a more prestigious club job for a professional. This was especially the case if the event happened to be the National Open. In this regard, McDermott's display in Philadelphia caught the attention of the Atlantic City Club and soon after, he became its head professional. This was most definitely a step up for John McDermott as the Atlantic City club was created, at the turn of the century, by local businessmen and hoteliers to attract the wealthy or "high end" clientele to the famous East Coast resort. Here he would have the chance of making a good living from giving lessons to a much wider and better off membership than at Merchantville: selling his hand-crafted clubs; and, crucially, as noted earlier, developing his game. It seemed as if John McDermott was truly on his way.

As a postscript to the U.S. Open, in August 1910, McDermott returned to the Cricket Club for the Philadelphia Open. This time he came out a winner when he beat four-time U.S. Open Champion, Willie Anderson, by a shot. His winning score for the 36-hole tournament was 146. Whether they liked it or not, the seasoned foreign pros would now have to contend with John McDermott. Further evidence of McDermott's rising status was also recorded in an article in the prestigious *New York Times* not long after the Philadelphia Open. It read,

> By winning the open championship of Philadelphia at the Philadelphia Cricket Club, J.J. McDermott has so impressed the amateurs of Philadelphia with the sterling worth of his game that a group of them have decided to send him to the open championship of the Metropolitan Association at Deal..................and to the Western Open Championship the following week.[26]

The words "so impressed the amateurs of Philadelphia" might be seen as a reminder of the professional's place in the golfing world. However, for the still teenage John McDermott, it was recognition of his recent achievements and in practical terms his expenses were guaranteed for the upcoming tournaments. At that stage, the Western Open was still a match-play tournament and he made an early exit. But at Deal, New Jersey, for the Metropolitan Open, it was a different story.

26 *The New York Times*, August 14, 1910.

The Deal Country Club on Jersey Shore was a prestigious venue and a regular holder of professional and amateur tournaments. It was also, at roughly 6500 yards in length, a serious test of golf. By now, the reporters were paying close attention to McDermott because of his talent, his youth and because he was an American taking on the foreign-born pros. And the galleries were taking an interest too. At the Metropolitan, McDermott captured the first- round headlines and he was referred to as, "The caddy boy professional at Merchantville Field Club who did the course in the startling figures of 71, three strokes under par."[27] In this, the first morning of the tournament, as was expected, the reigning U.S. Open Champion, Alex Smith, attracted most of the crowds. It was, however, a different story in the afternoon when it was reported that Smith, "was dropped like a hot potato and the entire gallery lionised the youngster."[28]

Perhaps the pressure got to McDermott as in the afternoon, he shot an 82, eleven worse than his morning round. But he and Smith were tied first after 36 holes on 153. And, he did recover the following day and shot a pair of highly creditable 75's. And in an effort to catch Smith who was playing ahead of him, it was reported that McDermott removed his customary jacket. But he still came up two short of Smith's winning total of 301. However, as well as the many references to his fine golf, it was McDermott's feisty temperament that was again reported on. Having finished later than Smith, and on hearing that he had come up short against the Scotsman for the second time that summer, his response was, "I'll get him yet."[29] The "caddy boy" tag stayed with McDermott and did him no harm as it was good copy for the newspapers who enjoyed the notion of the guy from the American caddy yard taking on the big boys. And, his performance at Deal more than justified the faith shown in him by his Philadelphia backers. He also took home $100 for his second- place finish.

As 1910 drew to a closed, a review in ***The Pittsburgh Press*** took a look at the bigger picture in terms of American golf as well as the playing performances that year. It painted a very positive picture and declared that "Thanks to the personality of President Taft, our first executive to take up the Royal and Ancient game, golf has made wonderful strides in these past two years." Taft was indeed an enthusiastic golfer and played regularly at the Chevy Chase Club in Washington. The article

---

27 *The Times Union,* August 26, 1910.

28 *Ibid.*

29 *The Brooklyn Daily Eagle,* August 27, 1910.

continued with a broader look at the development of golf, "It is no longer greeted with scoffing and irony and those who came to scoff have remained to play. While it is not generally known, there is a greater sum of money invested in the numerous links which dot the continent than the many league baseball grounds from Maine to California have cost."[30] The reference to William Howard Taft was appropriate, especially in regard to the suggestion in the review that golf was no longer a game just for the few. Because Taft was not just a "golf-playing- president," and in time, he called for more municipal courses to be built for those who "cannot pay costly club privileges."

Taft also declared that these courses should be funded by taxation: a daring program for a Republican president. It did take a while but in time, municipal courses became very much a feature of America's golfing landscape. In these early days, having golf attached to such headlines could only help popularize the game and indirectly aid John McDermott and the growing numbers in his profession. And in the same review, while much attention was devoted to the amateur champions of the year such as Chick Evans and W.C. Fownes, it was also recorded that "another item of importance was the work of Jack McDermott."[31] Undoubtedly what was capturing the attention of the Press and the wider golfing world, was that in the person of John McDermott, the United States now had someone who could stand up to the immigrant professionals who heretofore had dominated the game. As illustrated by his rivalry with the "invaders" during 1910, and how this was reported, this was a theme that ran throughout the year and would continue to do so in 1911.

30 *The Pittsburgh Press*, December 4, 1910.
31 *Ibid.*

# Chapter Three
# 1911 CHICAGO

With his new found status, John McDermott could look forward to 1911 with even greater self-assurance than he already had. In terms of official competition, however, there was not a great deal in the early months of this year. One tournament that did take place was the North and South at Pinehurst. And here, and in a sign of things to come for the year, Gilbert Nicholls was a runaway victor with the excellent scores of 68 and 73 for the 36-hole event. For whatever reason, McDermott did not play. He did, however keep his game sharp and early that year, he issued challenges to local pros in Philadelphia to 18- hole challenge matches for the sizeable sum of $1000. Robert Somers recorded that after three straight victories "the competition dried up."[32] As we saw when he challenged Alex Smith the previous year at the Philadelphia Cricket Club, McDermott was never short of confidence (or it seems money) when it came to backing himself against "all comers." The tournament calendar, such as it was, did not really get going until the second half of the year, starting with the U.S. Open in June. The Championship that year was held at the Chicago Club in Wheaton, on the outskirts of the city, and it was to prove a seminal moment in the history of American golf.

The Chicago Club was already part of American golfing royalty, having already hosted the U.S. Amateur and the U.S. Open of 1900 won by Harry Vardon. Vardon's victory added to the club's prestige but he would not be in Chicago this time. However, his brother Tom, who had recently joined the ranks of the immigrant professionals, would compete. The club was founded by Charles B. Macdonald, who also designed the course. It was the oldest in America and one of the five founding clubs of the United States Golf Association (USGA). MacDonald was born in Ontario and came from a wealthy family. This privileged background enabled him to attend university at St Andrews where he learned the game with the help of both

32 Somers, p 28.

Tom Morris Sr and Jr. He then brought his ideas back to Chicago and many see him as the father of American golf. A more measured view, however, came from Herbert Warren Wind who suggested that MacDonald may not have become "Mr American Golf," but he did "contribute more to the advancement of golf in American than any other person of his generation." [33] Whatever view is taken, MacDonald was a massive figure in early American golf and the Chicago Club was a fitting testament to his vision and expertise. Such a hallowed golfing environment, however, was unlikely to faze the 20 -year-old John McDermott.

The Chicago course was a true test of championship golf. It measured 6,605 yards in length with a par of 76 and it was "remarkably well bunkered and filled with natural hazards that lie in wait for the unwary."[34]. This par figure of 76 may seem high but we need to take into account the equipment available at that time, especially the ball, that saw, for example, the 429 yards 18th hole listed as a par five. Such a hole, however, would require two good shots to get home. In practice, McDermott, who was scoring in the low seventies, was deemed to be in good form as were Fred McLeod and Tom McNamara. Regarding these low scores the defending champion Alex Smith, dismissed the issue of form in practice rounds by saying, "It's the scoring when the strain of competition is on that tells."[35] As it happened, he was suffering from a stomach attack and a back spasm and neither he, nor the much- fancied McNamara would be a factor in the championship.

The conditions for the opening two rounds on June 23 were hot and dry and a total of 72 players took part, with 15 of these being amateurs. John McDermott had a wretched first round of 81 that saw him seven shots behind the 1907 champion, Alex Ross. He fought back, however, with the joint lowest round of the afternoon, a four under 72. His total of 153 saw him four back of joint leaders Ross and Fred McLeod. Tied with McDermott at this stage was Mike Brady who would have a big say in the championship. The following and final day saw somewhat different conditions with on and off rain. These conditions clearly affected Ross who struggled to an 81 and followed this with an afternoon 82. McDermott was playing with joint leader, McLeod and gained one stroke with a 75 to the 1908 champion's 76. This left him joint second on 228 with Gilbert Nicholls and only three back of the leader, McLeod. At this stage both Mike Brady and George Simpson were on 232.

---

33 Wind, p 27.

34 *The Brooklyn Daily Eagle*, June 19, 1911.

35 *The American Golfer*, August, 1911.

With one round to go, it is often the case that those starting earlier than the leaders have a distinct advantage. These players can post a score and put pressure on those who will finish later. Such was true in part at Chicago. For example, both Brady and Simpson shot one under rounds of 75 and so set a target of 307. What was a surprise, however, was the performance of the normally reliable Gilbert Nicholls who shot 81 and finished on 309. McDermott and McLeod were paired together but the former champion struggled badly and his final round of 83 left him one shot short of the required 307. McDermott also struggled and began his final round with a bogey six on the 468- yard opening hole. In rounds one and two he had picked up birdies on this hole. After this, his form was erratic with double bogey six at the short par- four fifth hole, being off-set by a 2 at the 140 yards ninth. In the end it came down to the par- five 18th that measured just 427 yards, but being played under the most intense pressure. Here McDermott secured the birdie four needed to match Brady and Simpson and so force the first three-way play-off in U.S. Open history. The 307 score of Brady, McDermott and Simpson was six shots better than Harry Vardon's winning total in 1900.

As with Philadelphia the previous year, the play-off was delayed until the following Monday due to the Blue Laws in Chicago. And, it was nicely poised as it would feature two young homebreds against yet another immigrant pro in George Simpson. Simpson came from Monifieth on Scotland's east coast and not too far from Carnoustie. Before emigrating to the United States, he held the Scottish Amateur title. Like all professionals at that time, his main income came from club duties but he was runner up to the amateur, Chick Evans, in the previous year's prestigious Western Open. For this finish, he received $100 as the leading professional. He may not have been the "home" favorite, but he was professional at the nearby Wheaton Club and so could count on support from his members.

The remaining play-off contestant was Michael Joseph "King" Brady, another member of the Boston/Irish clan. Brady, a few years older than McDermott, was born in Brighton Massachusetts in 1897 and like Tom McNamara, he too learned the game by caddying at Brookline. The Country Club had the very progressive policy of allowing caddies to play the course during the quieter times. Brady went on to play many exhibitions with John McDermott and in his own right had a fine career that saw him capture nine tour victories. Brady's trademark was his wonderful iron play and he is said to have given lessons to Tommy Armour when the Scotsman first came to the United States. History has shown us that Armour was one of the greatest iron players of all time. Like Tom McNamara, Brady was the "nearly man" of the U.S Open, never more so than at Brae Burn in 1919 when, with a final round of 80, he surrendered a five- shot lead to Walter Hagen and then lost the resultant play-off, 77 to 78

So, the stage was set to see if either Brady or McDermott could become the first native-born to win the National Open title. Brady, incidentally, carried only six clubs at a time when there was no limit to the permissible number of clubs. And yet before a ball was struck, McDermott took a decision that could have cost him the title. On the morning of the play-off, he was approached by a representative of the St Mungo Company. The parent firm was in Glasgow and was named after the patron saint of the city, St Mungo. However, it also had an outlet in New Jersey and its speciality was the "Little Colonel" golf ball that sold for 75 cents each. McDermott was offered $300 if he would use the ball in the title decider and he agreed, as success would see him double the first prize of $300. In those days, out of bounds consisted of just a one -shot penalty and at the par-five first hole, McDermott hit two "Little Colonels" out of bounds. He did manage a birdie four with this third ball but the resultant six was an inauspicious start to the day. Brady had a four and Simpson a five and so already, McDermott was two behind. He quickly recovered, however, and at the par four second, Brady's double bogey and Simpson's five, let him back into the match. His par there seemed to steady him and he completed the outward half in 39- just two over the card. In contrast, Brady and Simpson shot 43 and 44 for the same stretch, seemingly leaving McDermott in control of the play-off.

Winning the title, however, was not straightforward and a poor start to the back nine saw him drop three shots in the first four holes. As two of these were par fives, and holes where he might expect to pick up one birdie, this could have put the title in doubt. In contrast, Brady played this stretch in one under the card and picked up the four shots he had dropped to McDermott on the front nine. By now, Simpson was struggling and it became a two-man contest between the Irish/ Americans. It was then that McDermott showed his champion's credentials when he covered the remaining five holes in four shots each. These were all par fours except the 427- yard 18$^{th}$ hole which was a par five. With a one stroke lead over Brady, McDermott clinched the championship in style. After a perfect drive, he hit his second into 12 feet from the hole to set up a comfortable birdie four to Brady's par five. This was truly the finish of a champion and saw him sign for an 80 that was two ahead of Brady and six better than Simpson, who never really featured after the opening holes.

On paper the scoring was distinctly average but J.G. Davis, writing for *The Chicago Tribune,* put matters into context. He wrote, "As a championship display the performance was disappointing. There was a strong south westerly wind, the worst that can blow on the Chicago course, and this combined with the fact that all three players were under the strain of playing for the highest honor in professional golf in this country."[36] To Davis' observations, we can add that considering what was at stake for McDermott and Brady especially, it was understandable that the play-off would be a tense affair. Standing on the first tee that Monday morning, both men knew that one had the chance to make history by becoming the first American born man to win the U.S. Open. It was quite a prize.

In addition to the trophy, the gold medal, and the $300 first prize, McDermott also received the agreed similar cash amount from the St Mungo firm. And in an advertisement soon after, the company proclaimed how both the winner and runner-up of the U.S. Open had played the "Little Colonel" Green X ball. Apart from McDermott, George Simpson and Mike Brady had also been approached before the play-off, although it is unclear if Simpson accepted the offer or what Brady received for his runner-up finish. For Mc Dermott, however, business was business, and after the Championship was secure, he returned to playing his usual Rawlings Black Circle ball. His agreement with St Mungo was a "once off." And, in typically honest fashion, a few weeks after the play-off, McDermott sent a hand-written letter to the Rawlings Company explaining his decision.

> Gentlemen, in relation to your inquiry....................... the manufacturers of the colonel ball through their agent offered any of the three winning with their ball in the playoff three hundred dollars. I thought this chance was too good to lose. I only used the colonel ball in the playoff. If I had used the black circle ball, I should have had a few strokes better. I am now for using the black circle ball as I did throughout the open championship and shall continue to do so in all the tournaments and exhibition matches and when I go to Scotland. I consider the black circle the best ball ever made.[37]

36 *The Chicago Tribune*, June 27, 1911.

37 Eubanks

The fact that McDermott took the time to write to Rawlings about their "inquiry" suggests there may have been some form of agreement between the two parties. Perhaps in those early days of professional golf, it was just a verbal understanding rather than a written, binding, contract. What is clear is that McDermott believed changing his ball was a risk and judging by his opening two tee shots, he was right. But, as he suggests in his letter, the $300 on offer was too good to refuse, even if he may have won more comfortably had he stayed with the Rawlings ball. In any event, a few months short of his 20th birthday, John McDermott left the Chicago Club $600 richer. And as well as being the first "homebred" to win the title, he was also the youngest ever, a record that stands to this day.

The aftermath of McDermott's historic victory, provide some insights into where professional golf stood regarding newspaper coverage. It should be remembered that at this stage, newspapers ***were*** the mass media. It is also worth recalling that the amateur game usually occupied more column inches than its professional counterpart, and it would take Francis Ouimet's triumph two years later to truly put the game of golf on the front pages. In 1911, amateur championships were deemed to be more worthy of press coverage than the professional game. For example, for the U.S. Amateur Championship in September that year, *The New York Times* gave a number of columns to the victory of Britain's Harold Hilton over Fred Hereshoff at Apawamis. The detailed report included a hole -by- hole account of the 36-hole final and even made references to the content of Hilton's victory speech.[38] Nevertheless, there were responses in the print media to McDermott's win and some of these are instructive. For many outlets, a headline such as "Former Caddie Golf Champion," or "First American Born To Win It," followed by a brief report on the scoring, was enough. And another headline referenced his age, "Caddy, Pro Champion Not Yet Twenty One" [39] This report also referred to the help he received from head pro Walter Reynolds for whom he caddied at Aronimink. But there were exceptions to this line of reporting that made an attempt to explain in some detail, ***why*** and ***how*** McDermott won.

For instance, ***The Chicago Daily News*** gave considerable space to outlining the ebbs and flows of the play-off, even if the reporting was not always accurate. The report, for example, when focusing on McDermott's play through the green, recorded that there "was scarcely a flaw in his long game." Considering he started

38 *The New York Times*, September 17, 1911.
39 *The Brooklyn Daily Eagle*, June 27, 1911.

the round with two balls out of bounds from the first tee, such reporting did not give the reader the full story. The report, however, did highlight with a degree of accuracy the problems McDermott had on the greens. "McDermott's putting was the part of the game which prevented him making a more creditable medal score...............he was nervous and, on several occasions, failed to run down outs which almost a tyro could have made."[40] The report also commented on Brady's unusually poor iron play and how even Simpson's best friends did not give him much of a chance as "the former Scotch champion had a lame shoulder."[41] Such reporting would not match either that of Bernard Darwin or Grantland Rice, but it did at least go deeper than the figures returned by each player, especially those of McDermott.

Perhaps a more insightful report appeared in ***The Boston Herald*** which delved into the psychology of golf and how it may have impacted on the outcome at Chicago. "It began, "There are probably no two golfers in this or any other land so widely different as John J. McDermott, the open champion of the United States and Michael J. Brady...............McDermott has supreme confidence in his ability and he doesn't hesitate to tell everyone of his prowess....................Brady is sensitive and while, perhaps, over modest, it is a natural trait, surely not affected."[42] The report continued, "Two years ago Donald Ross said "Brady was a beautiful player but lacking the confidence that vastly helps in winning, not only in golf but in about every other sport."[43] Donald Ross was a widely respected and authoritative voice on the game and his words should not be seen as a criticism of Brady. Rather he was merely stating that in any age, supreme self-confidence is essential for a champion golfer, be it the more flamboyant approach taken by Hagen or, later on, the quieter inner belief of Bobby Jones.

Perhaps it was this lack of confidence that told against Mike Brady in Chicago or three years later at Midlothian when surrendered a five-shot final round lead and then narrowly lost out to Walter Hagen in a play-off. These occasions were the closest he came to winning the U.S. Open. In contrast, although not mentioning McDermott by name, Ross was suggesting that his personality was a help in achieving the game's great prizes. Certainly, he ruffled feathers as he did with Alex

---

40 *The Chicago Daily News*, June 27, 1911.

41 *Ibid.*

42 *The Boston Herald*, June 27, 1911.

43 *Ibid.*

Smith at Chicago the previous year and as he would again. But as a young man who had just won the National Open, John McDermott was not going to change his game or his personality, regardless of how some may have perceived him.

As we saw, Englishman, Gilbert Nicholls came very close at Chicago, finishing only two shots out of a play-off. Nicholls was yet another British-born professional to make his career in the United States. In his case, Nicholls came from the golfing heartland of Kent, on England's south east coast. He was a player with a fine pedigree who apart from his close call in Chicago, had already finished second in the U.S. Open of 1904 and 1907. In total he would enjoy five official tournament victories on tour. For much of the remainder of the golfing calendar, he and John McDermott were the names to watch out for. For example, at Englewood, just weeks after the U.S. Open, both contested the highly regarded Metropolitan Open. Even as far back as 1911, there was a tradition of holding an amateur-professional contest the day before the tournament started and this was the case here. When the tournament proper got under way, both Nicholls and McDermott were tied for the lead after 36 holes on 144. However, the final rounds saw Nicholls pull away and score a decisive victory over the field. His last round of 66 gave him a finishing score of 281, 11 under par. Reports suggested this was a "world record" as it beat Arnaud Massey's existing four round total of 284 at the French Open. Meanwhile, McDermott faded and finished up on 295. His prize for the four rounds was $25 while Nicholls took home $150 as the winner, plus an extra $30 for his 66.

For McDermott, however, there was a further "sting" apart from the disappointment of finishing so far behind Nicholls. This came in the form of a report on his behaviour in *The Brooklyn Daily Eagle*. The newspaper was quick to acknowledge his golfing prowess but believed that the newly-crowned U.S. Open Champion should act in a certain manner. It was reported that "Several times during the match he ventured remarks......that were in rather bad taste but youth is youth and a few more beatings such as were administered at the Englewood course should have a wonderful effect toward taming a rather too self-satisfied nature."[44] Clearly the writer could hardly contain his pleasure at the "beating" received at the hands of Gilbert Nicholls, but there is little doubt that the necessary confidence Donald Ross spoke of previously, in the case of John McDermott, regularly morphed into an unwelcome cockiness.

---

44 *The Brooklyn Daily Eagle*, July 16, 1911.

There were, however, also some positive reviews for McDermott in the aftermath of the Metropolitan Open. Ever since he burst onto the golfing scene, John McDermott's caddy background had been a great source of copy for American sports writers. The caddy yard story fed neatly into the homebred versus immigrant narrative that was so popular during this era. In this regard, *The Brooklyn Eagle,* perhaps balancing the earlier criticism of McDermott and his "bad taste," adopted this theme and claimed that the recently crowned U.S. Open champion had achieved hero status among American caddies. It wrote how McDermott, "rose from the ranks of caddydom, and they seem to feel he has vindicated them in the eyes of the world and given them a new right to live. It has always been the custom, to a certain extent at least, the make the caddy feel that he occupies the same position as the harmless, necessary cat."

And the piece continued to suggest that, "McDermott can feel he has the good wishes of every caddy in America when he has gone into the field of battle."[45] The suggestion that McDermott had given the American caddies a new "right to live" seems a little strong and comparing a caddy to a "harmless cat" hardly stands up to much scrutiny. John McDermott, himself, possessed certain skills which the members at Aronimink were happy to engage the services of, just a few years earlier. However, the idea that he may have been an inspiration to young caddies may not have been so far- fetched when graduates of the American caddy yard, such as Francis Ouimet and Walter Hagen, would soon follow in his footsteps and claim the U.S. Open title.

Despite the setback at Englewood, in August, McDermott, as defending champion, took the 36-hole Philadelphia Open at Whitemarsh with a score of 150. His prize here was $150 and the newspapers called it a "dollar a stroke." This victory brought a powerful tribute from the local *Philadelphia Inquirer*. Writing of McDermott, the account finished with, "His work in these recent tournaments has demonstrated that an American golfer is the equal of the Scotch players than whom there is supposed to be no better."[46] In this, and in many other words written of McDermott since Chicago, there was an unmistakeable and understandable sense of pride that the homebreds were a match for anyone. The following years would show this to be case.

45 *Ibid*, July 13, 1911.

46 *The Philadelphia Inquirer,* August 14, 1911.

The rivalry with Nicholls continued through August and September with a 72- hole stroke-play match arranged on a home and home basis and the press continued to play up the rivalry. The first 36 holes were to take place at McDermott's home club in Atlantic City and the second leg, a few weeks later, at Wilmington where Nicholls was the head pro. The newspapers billed this as a "world decider" even though McDermott was now the U.S. Open champion. One newspaper even described the second 36-holes as being for the "Professional Championship of the United States."[47] Nicholls led by four after the first 36 and at Wilmington, the scores were tied on 149. This left Nicholls the winner by four and for this he received a $100 prize for his victory at Atlantic City and the second $100 was split because of the tie at Wilmington. The match was good publicity for the professional game but McDermott's $50 after 72 holes of golf in two different locations, is an indication of how far the professional game had yet to go.

For the remainder of the year, John McDermott's name featured mostly in exhibition matches and in one of these, he beat Britain's George Duncan 3/2 in a 36-hole match at the Philadelphia Cricket Club. His victory was noted in many newspapers as being further proof of the native American professional's ability to handle his British counterpart. Duncan would go on to win the Open Championship in 1920. McDermott also embarked on a tour of Tennessee, Kentucky, and Virginia with Tom McNamara. He was clearly in demand and earning some money from such trips, to add to the income he derived from Atlantic City. However, as the year drew to a close, there was a salient newspaper report that shed light on certain realities for the U.S. Open Champion. This report celebrated McDermott's historic year as well as highlighting his roots, both past and present. It went on,

> That the district from which J.J. McDermott hails, New Jersey and Philadelphia, is keenly alive to the merits of his golf and anxious to give him encouragement, has been shown by the disposition on the part of golfers to subscribe liberally to a fund which will be used next year to finance his visit to Great Britain, where he will play against the best in the world, the meeting probably to be held at Muirfield in Scotland.[48]

The wording in the article may be a little verbose but it is commendable in highlighting the support ***for*** and ***goodwill*** towards John McDermott both in Atlantic

47 *The Evening Journal,* September 5, 1911.
48 *The Boston Globe*, November 26, 1911.

City and in his home town of Philadelphia. It also suggests, however, that despite earning a good income from his post at the Atlantic City Club, and his being U.S. Open champion with the consequent rewards, McDermott still needed financial support for a trip to Scotland. To be sure, such journeys over sea and land were long and might last a few weeks in total, but it was a reminder of how difficult it was for even the best players in the game to make serious money at this time. Regardless of these factors, McDermott himself was quick to express his gratitude for the support.

For many years, Harrison Townsend was secretary/treasurer of the Philadelphia Golf Association. He was very much behind the drive to finance the trip to Britain and he would later figure prominently, in the life of John McDermott. In a letter to him, the recently-crowned U.S. Open champion expressed his appreciation accordingly-

> Dear Sir- I wish, through you, to express to the golfers of Philadelphia my sincere appreciation of their great present to me, and my trip abroad. This is one of the greatest things ever done for a professional golfer, in fact, never having been done before in the United States. When I go abroad to compete in the principal events of the game of golf in Great Britain, I will do my utmost to represent the United States and Philadelphia to the best of my ability, both in play and deportment. Again, with renewed thanks to the committee and the subscribers to the fund, I remain, your very faithfully, JOHN J. McDERMOTT. [49]

In later years, McDermott would admit to being somewhat embarrassed by his lack of penmanship, but this letter to Harrison Townsend was both heartfelt and eloquent. However, what stands out most of all is how this was a "first" in American golf. McDermott would be the first homebred to compete in the Open Championship and the first to receive the necessary financial backing. This support was a mark of the impact his win at the U.S. Open had made on the consciousness of the American golfing public.

And there were plenty of celebratory end-of-season reviews, for it was such a momentous year in the history of American professional golf. Again J.G. Davis of *The Chicago Tribune* put the season into perspective. He wrote, "viewed through home spectacles the triumphs of J.J McDermott in the open championship of The United

---

49 *The Brooklyn Daily Eagle,* November 27, 1911.

States Golf Association was the most pleasing feature of a year replete with fine golf performances. It took thirteen years for home talent to come to the top and two home professionals landed, the second place going to M.J. Brady of Boston."[50] There was more than a touch of jingoism here but it was perfectly understandable and the reference to Mike Brady was well merited. There is no doubt that John McDermott would have been more than happy to see his fellow Irish-American mentioned in an appraisal of this historic year.

And further references to the Irish/American duo were found in reports of their immediate plans for the following season. The early months of the year usually saw the top players head for warmer territory to hone their games and make a few dollars by way of exhibitions. In this instance, Walter E. Murphy, in a piece in *The Boston Herald,* reported that

> Michael J. Brady........and John McDermott, the open champion of this country, will start on a tour of conquest the coming week through the South, the Southwest and the far West, that is scheduled to end shortly before the return of the robin to the North. It's a great combination of young American 'pros' beyond question the finest that could be drawn, and the pair will open the eyes of the golfer's world in remote places to the possibilities of the little fellows who carry around bags of clubs for grown ups. [51]

Here Murphy was again highlighting the caddie background of both Brady and McDermott and how the success of both, especially the new U.S. Open champion, could be a motivation for other American boys from similar origins.

50 *The Chicago Tribune*, December 31, 1911.
51 *The Boston Herald,* December 24, 1911.

# Chapter Four

# 1912 BUFFALO

The interest shown, at the end of 1911, in sending McDermott to contest the Open Championship at Muirfield dominated the golf headlines and as early as February 1912, the newspapers were full of stories about The Open in June of that year. *The Boston Journal* spelled out the significance of the trip in no uncertain terms. "For the first time in the history of professional golf "it proclaimed," an American professional will attempt to capture the open championship of Great Britain."[52] Even at this early stage of 1912, it was clear that the achievements of the first home-bred national champion had considerably elevated the confidence and expectancy level of the American golfing community. As for McDermott himself, he was relatively measured in his comments as to what lay ahead in Britain. "I hardly expect to win the title at my first attempt," he said, "but I will cause the English and Scotch professionals to realize that there are some golfers on this side of the Atlantic."[53] These comments were not as controversial as some made by the U.S. Open champion, but the fires burning within him regarding British golfing supremacy was never far below the surface.

Other newspapers picked up on the potential contest between the new homebred Americans and those from across the Atlantic. A particular theme that ran was the age difference between the American and British players. One headline read, "McDermott's play in Scotland will afford a contrast.............Abroad the leading golfers are men in their forties while on this side of the Atlantic, the best players are young men."[54] This mention of the older British golfers doubtless referred to the ageing, but still brilliant players such as Vardon and Ray. As we shall see these forty- plus British golfers, still had plenty of golf left in them. And just before his departure, many newspapers, such as *The Sun,* gave him a send-off, "Jack McDermott goes after British Honors. Native Bred American golfer sure he will finish

52 *The Boston Journal*, February, 1912.

53 *Ibid.*

54 *The Altoona Mirror*, March 18, 1912.

in the top flight."[55] And *The New York* ***Times*** noted the significance of McDermott's trip in so far as he was the first homebred to challenge for golf's greatest prize. "The presence of McDermott on the other side," it began, "will create a situation entirely new in the history of golf. Heretofore, the Britons have been accustomed only to annual visits from the Jacks and the Willies who learned the game in Scotland."[56] In Muirfield, McDermott would have to compete not only with the "Jacks" and "Willies" now living in the United States, but also Vardon, Ray, and the elites of British golf.

A more personal note, however, was struck by New Jersey's *Home News*. It reported, "Among the many notable Knights who were initiated in Columbus Hall yesterday was Jack McDermott who leaves to-morrow on the Victoria Louise, going to Muirfield, Great Britain. The professional golfer is a member of the Atlantic City Council.....The second and third degrees were conferred on him." And in a reference to golf, "He says is playing at the top of his game." The Knights in question were the Knights of Columbus, a staunchly Catholic welfare organization that would prove very important in the later career of John McDermott. It was hardly a coincidence that McDermott's presence at such a ceremony would take place the day before he prepared for such an important journey. It was, arguably, an affirmation of his strong Catholic faith to fortify him as he embarked on such a significant step in his golfing career.

McDermott left for Scotland almost a month before the Open began and the early signs were good as evidenced by a letter from the Victoria Louise to his friend Mike Brady. McDermott had hoped that Brady would join him on the trip to Scotland and lend support to American efforts in the quest to bring back the claret jug. However, Brady, at this stage, had a dread of seasickness and declined to travel. There were no such fears for McDermott and he wrote, "ocean just like a pond: I never had a feeling of seasickness."[57] He also told Brady that he was swinging his clubs each day and even hitting some balls from the deck into the Atlantic. His period of acclimatization to British conditions was considerable and it included rounds at many famous locations including, Westward Ho, Deal, and Sandwich. All three were links courses with the latter two being Open Championship venues. It seemed as if nothing was being left to chance in McDermott's efforts to mount a challenge at Muirfield.

---

55 *The Sun*, May 6, 1912.

56 *The New York Times*, May 6, 1912.

57 *The Boston Evening Transcript*, May 24, 1912.

Meanwhile, back home his supporters in New Jersey were generally optimistic about his chances. *The Brooklyn Daily Eagle* reported that "The Atlantic City golfers are very confident that their professional, young J.J. McDermott, now in England, will give a good account of himself in the British open championship, not only because of his merits as a golfer, but because of his knowledge of sandy golf acquired in playing for two years at the seaside links of the Jersey resort." And the article continued, "Other American golfers have not had that acquaintance with turf resembling the British grass and they have come to grief."[58] Others, however, were not so sure and pointed to the reality of this young U.S. Open Champion playing against the likes of Vardon, Ray and Taylor on their home turf. It was true that the Atlantic City course was located by the sea but to suggest it was like a true links course, as in linking the arable land to the sea, was not really correct. There were many courses in the United States, such as Shinnecock Hills, that were also situated by the sea, but that did not have the same turf as a true links course. Atlantic City may have had a form of sandy turf but it was not the equivalent of what John McDermott would contend with at Muirfield. And perhaps more relevantly, he would not have encountered the same winds he was likely to face in the east of Scotland. The stage was set for a battle between the very young American champion and the vastly more experienced greats of the British game.

Muirfield, on Scotland's east coast, was the oldest recognized golf club in the world and it had already hosted the Open on four occasions. The links measured just short of 6500 yards and was seen as the fairest test on the championship rota. John McDermott had plenty of time to become used to British conditions, and in his planning for the Championship there was no sign of what lay ahead. As part of his preparation, McDermott teamed up at Muirfield with Jack White in a match against Arnaud Massey and local man Ben Sayers. The company he was playing with was befitting for the U.S. Open Champion as both White and Massey were former Open winners and local veteran and renowned club designer, Sayers, had finished second in 1888. It was a close match and the McDermott/White combination came out on top by 2/1. Their better ball of 68 was a very fine score over the Muirfield links. And in an article for *The Boston Evening Transcript*. J.G. Anderson reported of McDermott's practice rounds that "His medal scores at Muirfield have never been above 80 and he has made four 71's.................I have never seen so much confidence." [59]

58 *The Brooklyn Daily Eagle*, June 11, 1912.
59 *The Boston Evening Transcript*, July 3, 1912.

However, when the real action started it was a different story in every sense of the word as it was reported that McDermott "alienated some of the locals with his cocky attitude but was soon put in his place when he shot 91 and did not qualify."[60] In contrast to McDermott's alleged "cocky attitude," however, the London *Daily News* portrayed the pre-championship McDermott in a very different light. "You can tell British golfers,"He said, "that I shall not be disappointed if I don't carry your championship with me back to the States. I am here for a golfing education and shall be content to pick up a few wrinkles."[61] And, an education and a few wrinkles were just what he got.

Despite a 7.30 a.m. start, McDermott was followed by a large local gallery who were, no doubt, anxious to see the American champion in person. But a dropped shot at the par three first hole seemed to unsettle McDermott and mistakes became commonplace after that in his outward half. The apex of his misfortunes then came at the seventh. This hole was bordered on the left- hand side by a "dyke wall" (a very thick wall) that separated the links from the Archerfield Estate. Here Dermott was out of bounds three times with all his tee shots going left over the wall. It would have been four but for the wall saving McDermott's ball from a similar fate. The hole cost him an eight. This leftward shot, especially in windy conditions, could be a problem for McDermott. It even emerged when he was successful as in Chicago and Buffalo. McDermott also putted poorly in an outward half of 48 shots. However, in the afternoon round he fought hard and improved by ten shots. In the event, in tough conditions, his two-round total of 172 was only four shots outside the qualifying limit and it was very much a question of "what might have been" but for the first round of 91. As it turned out, the two "older men" men who would later feature so prominently in McDermott's career, Ray and Vardon, dominated the Championship proper. Ted Ray won with a score of 295 that was four shots better than his friend and rival.

For McDermott, the experience of finishing on a score of 91 in the Open Championship was mortifying, especially considering the support, both moral and financial, he received from his home city of Philadelphia. And one report, at least, referred to McDermott as having let down his home city. Under the heading, "American Golfer Fizzles," *The Philadelphia Inquirer* went on to report, "Alas for the high hopes of American golfers, especially the thousands in this city

60 *The Golf 100*, 1912.
61 *The Daily News*, June 20, 1912.

and vicinity, many of whom put up the money to send Johnny McDermott to England to capture the British Championship." The piece went on to refer to the U.S. Open Champion as "Bully" McDermott but it is not clear if this referred to his sometimes-abrasive temperament or not. And the report ended by suggesting that McDermott's problems at Muirfield were psychological rather than physical and quoted the "ancient adage that every man fights best in his own township."[62] Apart from the obvious error in reporting that local golfers contributed financially in sending McDermott to England rather than Muirfield in Scotland, the article does capture some of the disappointment felt by Philadelphians and golfers further afield. However, given his remarkable talents, it was rather facile to suggest that John McDermott could only play in his own back yard. A creditable showing in the French Open the following week confirmed this.

Further commentary came from Ben Sayers, who believed that McDermott had exhausted his strength with too much practice while other claimed that he was not prepared for the severe weather that was unlike anything he experienced during the championship lead-in. Such views can be classed as possible explanations but there was definitely criticism and from some quarters at least, it was severe. This was especially the case with England's Harold Hilton. At this stage, Hilton was one of the most successful players in the game and, in his regular newspaper columns, one of its most powerful voices. He was twice Open champion, a three -time British Amateur winner, and he had also won the U.S. Amateur plus a host of other titles. He was dismissive of McDermott's performance at Muirfield. "McDermott," he said" who came all the way from the United States, has only himself to blame for this terrible debacle as his play was puerile. He is an infant at golf."[63] Describing the American champion as a golfing "infant" was harsh in the extreme and unusual, as champions rarely spoke unkindly of each other, at least not publicly. But Hilton, with all his success, saw The United States as a nation of golfing inferiors and this was not the only occasion that he put down an American player.

And some of the criticism came from home. In an extremely anti- McDermott' piece, *The Boston Evening Transcript* ran a headline "How McDermott Was Deluded." This article suggested that in practice, McDermott was conceded and accepted putts in the two- to- four foot- range and that his reported practice scores were inflated as a result. And it further suggests that such lack of practice in holing

62 *The Philadelphia Inquirer*, June 22, 1912.
63 *The Brooklyn Daily Eagle*, June 25, 1912.

out led to McDermott missing many putts of this range in the qualifying rounds. On the other hand, an eminently reliable witness told a different story. Writer and amateur golfer, J.G Anderson later recalled how, "In one fourball match wherein he and I played against Arnaud Massy and Andrew Kirkaldy, McDermott went round in 71, holing every putt. That was the day before the qualifying round for the championship."[64] Having witnessed McDermott's play at first hand, Anderson's recollections must be taken seriously. However, the fact is that McDermott did miss a number of short putts in his first round of 91. In regard to his putting, John McDermott developed a very particular style on the greens. He addressed the ball with both his heels touching and some years later, this stance would be popularized by Bobby Jones. McDermott could not have achieved what he did without being a good putter, but it is debatable how reliable this narrow stance was with the wind blowing on seaside terrain. Many might argue that a wider stance would provide a more secure base.

In terms of further commentary on his performance, not everyone was as harsh as Hilton, and *The Boston Evening Transcript*. For example, the British correspondent of *The American Golfer* struck a different tone. He wrote of the difficulty Americans faced when they crossed the Atlantic, "They are in a strange country, on courses quite different from their own, and so they are, to some extent, handicapped. But apart from that, they are opposed to much bigger and stronger fields then they are at home......I am writing this sympathetically, for I should like to see the Americans do better than they are doing when they are over here."[65] This more balanced reporting highlights some of the problems that faced American golfers but the strange conditions and the stronger fields hardly explained a disappointing round of 91 from the U.S. champion, especially when we consider McDermott's extensive preparation for the examination.

Later, J.G. Anderson shed some more considered insight as to what may have contributed to McDermott's performance. Anderson was a highly rated amateur from Winged Foot who was twice runner up in the National Amateur Championship. He also won the French Amateur title on two occasions. And apart from a successful business career, he was a highly respected writer who contributed many golf columns to journals and the national newspapers, on both sides of the Atlantic. He also competed (without much success) at Muirfield in 1912 and so was well

64 *The Sun And New York Press*, April 17, 1916.
65 *The American Golfer,* August, 1912.

placed to witness McDermott's demise. Anderson recalled how McDermott's first qualifying round tee-time was at 7.30 am and that after an overly intensive practices session, he stood in the cold for 15 minutes awaiting the starter's call. Anderson and others tried to persuade him to step inside for a time but, perhaps because of nerves, McDermott refused. This incident, according to Anderson, contributed in no small way to his morning round. [66]

Anderson also recalled how during the Open, McDermott visited him in his room on several occasions, initially to say how determined he was to win and bring the title back to America, and then later to say how distraught he was at his performance. At this stage, McDermott just wanted to get the boat home as soon as the Open was over, but Anderson persuaded him to compete in the French Open the following week at La Boulie. La Boulie was described by some as the "St Andrews of France" and the Championship attracted a top-class field that included Vardon, Braid and Taylor. McDermott began nervously with two topped drives but he recovered to shoot a respectable 75 and after that played steadily with rounds of 74, 70, and 74. This was good enough for a total of 293 and a fifth- place finish just four shots behind the home winner, Jean Gassiat, who was one shot ahead of Vardon. What was significant, however, was that McDermott had shown that he could play well outside of America, even if it was not on links turf. Later, Anderson recalled McDermott's gratitude for the advice that directed him to France. "The play in the French championship, so he has told me many times since, gave back to him the confidence that had been his before the British Open Championship and enabled him to win the American championship at Buffalo that same year."[67]

The eighteenth U.S. Open was held on August first and second, 1912, at the Buffalo Country Club, New York. The club had its origins in 1899 near Delaware Park but in 1901, relocated to a site near the border between the city of Buffalo and Amherst. A clearly ambitious club, the committee hired Walter. J. Travis to re-design the course in 1910 and 1911 aiming to attract a prestigious tournament. Travis was an apposite choice for this task with an impeccable golfing pedigree. Originally from Australia, he became a naturalized American and, in 1904, became the first U.S. golfer to win the British Amateur Championship. He also won the U.S. Amateur on three occasions and finished second in the National Open in 1901. In addition, Travis founded, published, and wrote for, ***the American Golfer.*** His talents

66 *The Sun*, April 17, 1916.
67 *Ibid.*

also included golf course design and as well as remodelling Buffalo, he did a similar job at Columbia Country Club prior to its hosting the U.S. Open of 1921. And the famed Pine Valley also benefited from his influence.

The aim of Travis and the Buffalo committee was quickly achieved and the growing popularity of the game, and the National Championship, can be gauged by the fact that a record number of 128 entrants competed. Absent from this list, however, were any professionals from across the Atlantic, but this was not due to any lack of effort on the part of the host club. For, in an attempt to give the Championship as much prestige as possible, "the Buffalo Club sent alluring notices of the event to the famous professional golfers across the water," however. "these invitations were not accepted because the British talent....can earn more money at home than they could here during July and August. " And *The Boston Globe* also reported that "in former years as well as this year they have been approached, and the sums of money demanded were quite out of proportion to the service they possibly could give."[68] The writer does not specify if the demands of the British-based professionals were in the form of appearance money or guaranteed income from exhibition matches. However, if the report is accurate, it seems remarkable that Britain's professional golfers would require a financial guarantee to compete in the U.S. Open. Perhaps it was an indication that at this stage, 1912, the U.S. Championship was not highly rated across the water in the way that "The Open" was.

As for the test that awaited the players, what was notable about Buffalo was that for the first, and only time, a U.S. Open course contained a par 6. This was the 606 yards tenth hole. Otherwise, the lay-out, at 6326 yards of good length. The course was also balanced with four par threes, and six par fours measuring under 350 yards. However, apart from the par 6, there were also two par fives measuring over 500 yards that for this era was considered very long. The par for the course was 74.

The build-up to the Championship received a great deal of press coverage, and one newspaper, *The Buffalo Evening News*, labelled the event as "The Best in History" for two reasons. First, the aforementioned largest ever number of entrants. And secondly, what might be described as a form of American golfing "nativism" that had gained some currency in the media since John McDermott's success the previous year. The article read, "This year there is going to be tremendous rivalry

68 *The Boston Globe*, July 28, 1912.

between the golfer's born and raised in this country, the homebreds, as called, and the golfers who originally came from the other side of the Atlantic, the English and Scotch professionals, who came by their ability in large measure through natural inheritance." The piece then went on to claim that "McDermott's victory in 1911 compelled its recognition by the British professionals now resident in the United States."[69] The writer raised a questionable theory that the British professional's skill was as a result of "natural inheritance," questionable in the sense that this negates the idea that a great deal of hard work went into honing the skills of the English and Scottish pros. As for the rivalry between the homebreds and the imports, there was definitely some merit in this argument and nobody was more vocal in this regard than John McDermott who was either given or adopted the banner of the man who was not afraid to take on the British and Scottish professionals, either on or off the course. Of course, all of this provided great copy for the newspapers and was a colorful backdrop to the Championship. The favorites going into the contest were the "Irish/American" trio of McDermott, Brady and McNamara with former champion, Scotsman, Alex Smith, also fancied, as was relative newcomer, England's Jim Barnes.

With such a large field and with two rounds on the first day, play began at 6.30 a.m. and leading the way after round one were Mike Brady, Dan Kenney and former champion, England's George Sargent, each with 72. McDermott was neatly placed on 74 along with a large group that included Tom McNamara. Alex Smith, who shot 77, was not among the first- round leaders, but he repaired the damage that afternoon with the best round of the day, a 70 that saw him tied for the 36-hole lead on 147 with Mike Brady and the lesser known, P.F. Barrett. McDermott made a steady start to his defense with a level par 74 and after a second round of 75, was two shots behind the leaders on 149. Walter Travis, who designed the course, led the amateurs with a very creditable 152.

The final day for John McDermott began with a replay of his experience when winning the title at Chicago the previous year. We can recall that on the first hole of the Monday play-off, he hit two "Little Colonel'' golf balls out of bounds with his first two strokes. In Buffalo his opening hole of the third round saw him repeat the process (not with 'Little Colonel's) and with the two penalty shots, record a six. Both tee-shots went left and it was this shot that caused McDermott problems during

69 *The Buffalo Evening News*, July 24, 1912.

his career. At different times, newspaper reports referred to these shots as "pulls" or "hooks" but the final outcome was the same. This shaky start contributed to an outward 40 but a superb homeward nine of 34 saw him card a 74. The leader after three rounds was Mike Brady who was steadiness personified with rounds of 72, 75, 73 and his aggregate score of 220 was three better than McDermott and four ahead of Alex Smith.

The final round began disastrously for third round leader Brady. He started, 5-6-5, on three par four holes and ended the day with a 79. The big move in the final round was made by Tom McNamara who shot a five under par 69 that constituted a new course record. John McDermott, however, was playing a few holes behind McNamara and perhaps this was an advantage as it helped the reigning champion know exactly what was required down the closing stretch. As it was, McDermott went out in the 35 and led by three shots. His play on the back nine was almost as faultless and he finished with a 71 for 294 and a two -stroke victory over McNamara. His only blemish came at the final hole when another pull (this time his second shot) cost him a bogey. Brady and Smith finished next on 299 and Walter Travis tied for tenth place and was the leading amateur on 307.

McDermott's first prize was $300 and continuing on the "nativist" theme, September's edition of *The American Golfer* recorded that "of the players 'in the money' – the first ten- no less than seven learned the game in this country." This theme was also taken up by some of the wider print media with one report reading, "The Irish yesterday beat the Scotch at their own game- golf."[70] And further evidence of this refrain was found in the local *Buffalo News* which, in reference to the first four places, reminded its readers that "Alex Smith has never been accused of over fondness for professionals of home manufacture, so to see him wedged in between three such domestic articles pleases friends of the latter greatly." It will be recalled that at Chicago in 1910. McDermott and Alex Smith had words and clearly these exchanges, and perhaps other comments by Smith, had not been forgotten by some journalists. At all events, McDermott was champion for the second year running and this was the third successive year that nobody had beaten his 72-hole total in the U.S. Open.

70 *The Buffalo Enquirer*, August 3, 1912.

John McDermott's poised finish- note the elegant jacket in which he often played (courtesy Merion Golf Club).

When writing of McDermott's successful title defense, Robert Somers suggested that, "There seemed to be no limit to what he might accomplish. He was doing well financially: Clubs were marketed under his name, he endorsed balls, played exhibition matches, gave lessons and invested his money. The world was a lovely place."[71] The clubs he designed and marketed were particularly noteworthy as these included, "Drivers and a Speciality of Brassies With Ivory Faces." In addition, he marketed his "Famous Mashies...Models of His Own."[72] But despite all of this, John McDermott was already thinking further afield than his home country and championship.

71 Somers, p 30.

72 Merion G.C. Archives.

John McDermott with the 1912 U.S. OpenTrophy (courtesy Merion Golf Club).

Flushed with his success, in the aftermath of the U.S. trophy presentation, McDermott declared that he would definitely travel to Britain the following year in an attempt to win The Open and atone for his poor showing at Muirfield. And it would appear that he was not alone in his desire to become the first American-born player to win golf's greatest prize. Even with his tournament winnings and other sources of income, the cost of a lengthy stay across the Atlantic was not inconsiderable for the American Champion. So, it was welcome when a benefactor materialized as the following report confirmed. "In McDermott's case the financial end of next year's visit to the British Open need cause him no worry. He was told by an amateur golfer of his district that if he won the American Open at Buffalo, the funds for another trip abroad for him next year would be provided."[73] America had shown it could produce a golfer who was capable of maintaining the nation's golfing honor at home. Now, it appeared, that every effort must be made for America to prove that it also had a golfer who could triumph in the home of golf.

If McDermott's instinct was that he wanted to prove himself at the home of golf, it appears he was right in the sense that at least one influential voice from across the Atlantic poured scorn on his achievements at Buffalo. At this time, and for many years after, the most powerful golfing journal in Britain was *Golf Illustrated*. When reporting on McDermott's latest U.S. Open triumph it claimed that,

> It is difficult to know what construction to place on the result of the United States open championship. J.J. McDermott, who failed to survive the qualifying rounds of the British championship at Muirfield...........has now gained the honors of his own country for the second year in succession. Such condition of affairs suggests that any one of about 60 Englishmen, Scotsmen, Irishmen and Frenchmen, might have beaten McDermott if the field of players had not consisted entirely of men associated with American clubs.

Dripping, as it undoubtedly was, with condescension, the report was firmly put down by A.W.Tillinghast, who reproduced it in his regular column for *The Philadelphia Record.*[74] The sentiments expressed were, nevertheless, a further reminder of the rivalry that existed between the home of golf and the aspiring American professionals, especially the homebreds of whom McDermott was now the leader.

However, McDermott had more pressing matters on his mind after his victory as the months of August and September were busy months in the professional's very limited golfing calendar. Eight days after Buffalo he faced Gil Nicholls in a play-off for the prestigious Philadelphia Open: a tournament in which McDermott had enjoyed success in the past. The play-off was as a result of a tie between Nicholls and McDermott in the original event on July 18 when the pair tied on 149 for the 36 holes. Here, with Nicholls safely in the clubhouse and seemingly assured of victory, McDermott chipped in for a birdie three at the final hole to catch Nicholls. Because of a busy schedule, the play-off was held over until August and this time, Nicholls made no mistake when he beat McDermott by four shots, 71-75. The expectation

73 *The Boston Evening Transcript*, August 6, 1912.
74 *The Philadelphia Record*, August 25, 1912.

now surrounding John McDermott was expressed in a newspaper headline following the play-off that read, "McDermott Loses Golf Championship To Nicholls By Four Strokes."[75]

Shortly after this, attention turned to the prestigious Western Open at the Idlewild Country Club, Chicago, and here McDermott missed out on an excellent chance of victory. In his final round of 79 he gave up six shots to the eventual winner, MacDonald Smith, whose score of 73 saw him secure the title on 299. McDermott finished third on 303. Just days later, however, McDermott gained some revenge when at the same venue, he beat Smith 3/2 in a 36-hole challenge match for a $200 purse. Despite it being match-play, scores were kept and McDermott shot 76-77 and Smith, 77-79. The match was billed as an East versus West contest because of McDermott's Atlantic City base and Smith playing out of Del Monte, California. The local *Chicago Tribune* reported that there was a "fair size gallery and there was quite a little wagering on the result."[76] It was a notable feature of the era that apart from the few big tournaments and championships on the calendar, challenge matches and exhibitions were a vital part of the leading professional's life.

As the 1912 golf season drew to a close, professional golf in America was riding on the crest of a wave, largely due to McDermott's success in the U.S. Open. And even at this early stage, attention turned to what many saw as the next step in the homebred's development- success in the 1913 Open Championship. This was billed in advance as a "World Championship" as not only would all the top British professionals be present at Hoylake, for the first time many Americans also planned to travel. Indeed, the word "crusaders" was used to describe the American pros who planned to make the journey. In this regard, John McDermott, clearly having recovered from his embarrassment at Muirfield, saw fit to lay down a challenge to Harold Hilton, who was so dismissive of his performance in the Open Championship.

Hilton was also critical of American courses in comparison to those in Britain. McDermott's challenge took place at the 1912 U.S. Amateur Championship at Wheaton, Chicago. Hilton was defending champion but made an early exit in the championship that was won by American, Jerry Travers. Perhaps Hilton's surprise defeat, allied to the fact that McDermott had won the National Open at Wheaton that summer, encouraged the American champion to confront the Englishman. In

75 *The Philadelphia Inquirer*, August 11, 1912.
76 *The Chicago Tribune*, September 29, 1912.

any event, it was reported that, "McDermott, walking the course with H.H. Hilton, the famous English amateur, remarked to the visitor that the putting greens of the Chicago C.C. were as good as any that could be found in England. Hilton smiled." The report then continued, "McDermott, who has suffered from the pen of H.H. Hilton.............told the Englishman that the best players on his side of the water, had little or nothing in their golf bags which could not be found in the receptacles for golf clubs of the experts in the professional class in America. Hilton smiled again."[77] When the verbosity of the report as in "receptacles for golf clubs" is laid aside, the message was unmistakable- the American pros now had the confidence to take on the British professionals, on either side of the Atlantic. It is not clear how appreciative the other homebreds, such as Brady and McNamara, were of McDermott's fighting talk, but the newspapers loved it, even if not all agreed with it.

77 *The Boston Globe*, October 27, 1912.

# Chapter Five
# 1913 SHAWNEE AND BROOKLINE

At the start of 1913, life could not have looked better for John McDermott. He was a double U.S. Open Champion, and he was making money from exhibitions. McDermott was also in demand as a clubmaker from golfers anxious to have clubs from America's finest player, and he had a secure and happy position at the Atlantic City Club. In addition, the promises made after his win at Buffalo materialized when, in March 1913, the local Massachusetts Golf Association (MGA) displaying its pride in his achievements, and those of Tom McNamara, started a fund to help send McDermott and McNamara to the Open Championship at Hoylake. This was significant, as bodies, such as the MGA, were essentially amateur-centred, and not known for supporting the professional game. Subscriptions were limited to $2 and it was reported that "All the clubs are taking an active interest and there should not be any trouble in getting together sufficient funds for the trip."[78] It was yet another sign of recognition for the double National Open Champion, that his home Association wanted John McDermott, along with Tom McNamara, to travel to Britain and perhaps become the first American-born golfer to win the Open title.

At this stage in the development of professional golf in America, there was no organized tour from which players could make a decent living. The PGA was not formed until 1916 and it would be the 1920's and particularly the 1930's before a tournament circuit would emerge. For the top players, there were exhibition and challenge matches and then there was mainly the National Open- the prestigious Western Open- the Metropolitan Open- and the North and South tournament. Nevertheless, early in the year, there were some organised tournaments, usually held in the South with its warmer climate. One of these was held in February 1913

78 USGA Archives, letter dated March 1, 1913.

at the Augusta Country Club, and here, McDermott came in second in the 36-hole tournament. His scores of 79-73 were three shots behind Fred McLeod's winning total of 149. McLeod was a figure of substance in the world of golf. Another one of the Scottish-born professionals, he won the U.S. Open title in 1908 as well as a number of other tournaments. And, as we saw, only a final round 83 prevented him from winning the U.S. title in 1911, the occasion of McDermott's first victory. For John McDermott, however, apart from the defense of his U.S. Open title in September, the event that most occupied his mind in the first half of 1913, was the Open Championship at Hoylake. He was determined to make up for the bitter disappointment of his display at Muirfield the previous year.

Hoylake is one of a number of championship links courses in the greater Liverpool area including, Royal Birkdale, Southport & Ainsdale and Hillside. It was also the home club of McDermott's nemesis, Harold Hilton. In the lead-up to the Open, McDermott showed good form when he played an exhibition at the Royal Mid-Surrey Club. Here he partnered Tom McNamara to a 6/5 win over Mike Brady and S.H. Fry. Brady had also made the trip to play at Hoylake. McDermott's individual score of 68, with a back nine of 31, impressed the locals and he was seen as one to watch for the Open. That he was a feared invader was evident from a newspaper article that appeared after the Championship. It was written, appropriately, by ***Niblick***, who told his readers that he "was warned some time ago by a very fine judge of the game to look out for McDermott in the championship and really at one time so well was he doing it seemed as if the warning had not been issued without just reason. McDermott, however, fell away somewhat in his short game in the second afternoon and the fears of an American victory soon dissipated."[79]

Before the Championship itself began, however, there was the matter of qualification and this was no easy task for even the best of players. Because of the very large entry of 269 players, qualifying was held over three days with only 20 making it through on each day. McDermott was out on the second day and while his scores of 79 and 80 were at the back of the field, he was only seven shots behind the leading qualifier, Laurie Ayton on 152. With the intense pressure of qualifying over, he found his game in the Championship proper, and in the third round it looked, for a time, as if he might make a real challenge.

79 *Illustrated Sporting and Dramatic News*, June 13, 1913.

In those days, the Open was played over two days and after rounds of 75 and 80, McDermott lay eight shots behind leader, Ted Ray. The final day began in appalling conditions with *The Glasgow Herald* recording that, "When play began in the third round at nine o'clock, a drenching rain was driven along the course by a gale." Eventual winner J.H. Taylor, as he waited in the press tent to tee off, declared that "Golf under such conditions is a fiasco"[80] And Ireland's Michael Moran, who would finish fourth, began with a 10 at the 420 yards first hole. Conditions did improve a little but McDermott played the front nine in an excellent 36 and threatened to be involved in the finish. This threat was recognized later by Harold Hilton who had come to regard McDermott in a different light than he did a year previously after Muirfield.

Hilton was a regular contributor to newspapers and in *The Sheffield Daily Telegraph* he wrote of McDermott's bad fortune on the second nine. In the third round," Hilton wrote, "he was the one player who appeared at all likely to catch Taylor and Ray.............and when going to the fourteenth hole his score, at that stage was better than Ray and within a shot or two of Taylor." The fourteenth hole at Hoylake, named "Field," measured 485 yards long, and as a par five presented an opportunity for McDermott to pick up a shot. It was certainly reachable in two but as Hilton explained, it was to prove his undoing. He continued, "the fourteenth hole was disastrous to him, and the disaster was not his own fault as he hit a beautiful second shot which passed within a yard or two of the pin, but which had the misfortune to trickle on until it found the bunker beyond the green.[81] From here, McDermott took six and even though it was just one shot dropped, it appeared to stop his momentum and he finished with a round of 77.

Despite his back nine, McDermott was one of only five players to break 80 on a very tough final day. However, a last round 83 saw any slim hopes of victory vanish. For McDermott, Hoylake represented a considerable improvement on the previous year and he finished tied fifth, 11 shots behind the winner J.H. Taylor's score of 304. At this stage, this was the best ever finish by an American player in the Open and it was a portent of things to come in the following decades when Hagen, Jones, and others, won the claret jug. This was Taylor's final Open triumph and he received £50 first prize money- approximately $130. For his efforts, McDermott got £7/10s or a little less than $20. But it was, at least, a creditable performance.

---

80 *The Glasgow Herald*, June 25, 1913.

81 *The Sheffield Daily Telegraph*, September 19, 1913.

Overall, McDermott's effort drew praise from both sides of the Atlantic with his first-day round of 75 and the first nine 36 in his third round, being seen as proof that he could indeed play links golf. It also seemed that in the wind, McDermott had managed to avoid the damaging left-bound shots, especially from the tee, that had cost him dearly at The Open the previous year. Apart from Hilton's sympathetic comments on his bad luck, McDermott's improvement on Muirfield was especially noted by Ernest Lehmann witing in the leading British golf journal, ***Golf Illustrated***. He wrote of his first round, "McDermott, the American Champion, recognised by all as the most dangerous competitor from the States, gave a display of his true form, and by returning a brilliant 75 showed that his display at Muirfield last year was no criterion of his real powers."[82] And, of his third round Lehmann continued, "McDermott with his extraordinary figures for the first thirteen holes gave everyone a severe fright and showed what a grand golfer he is. He had those holes in an average of 4's!"[83] For only his second tilt at the Open, Hoylake represented a major advancement by McDermott and many saw it as a stepping stone to his eventual success in the Championship.

After Hoylake, McDermott joined Tom McNamara, Mike Brady and Alex Smith and again headed for France, this time to play a team of French professionals in a match arranged earlier that year. This was not just seen as an exhibition match and while it would be an exaggeration to say it was a forerunner of the Ryder Cup, the trans-Atlantic contest was taken seriously, evidenced by the fact that as part of the collection to send McDermott and McNamara to Hoylake, the MGA also asked contributors to bear in mind the expense incurred for the French trip after the Open. The seriousness with that the Americans took the contest could also be seen in the naming of two substitutes, Gilbert Nicholls and Alex Campbell. In the event all the American effort was in vain. The French fielded a strong line-up that included former Open Champion Arnaud Massey and the visitors lost all 6 matches, two in foursomes and four in singles.

After France, it was back home and McDermott, for the third time, won the Philadelphia Open with a score of 305. This was three better that of runner up Isaac Mackie, who was another of the Scottish professionals who had migrated to The United States. And McDermott's form continued, in part at least, when he played in the Metropolitan Open at Garden City, New York, in mid-August. Here he

---

82 *Golf Illustrated*, UK, July 4, 1913.

83 *Ibid.*

looked to be well on course for another win after rounds of 71-71-73. Before the final round, when he led Alex Smith by one shot, the simmering feud between the Scotsman and McDermott re-emerged. It was reported that "So keen was the rivalry between McDermott and Smith that they could not avoid a wordy clash during the intermission. The result was a wager between the two as to their relative positions at the finish. Some one asked McDermott if Alec was getting his nerve whereupon the doughty homebred said that he had more nerve than any three Smiths."[84] As it turned out the homebred's nerve was not that good and a disastrous final round of 79 saw him finish on 294, three shots behind Alex Smith's 291, and two back of Tom McNamara. And, it was the ultimate test of nerve, putting, that let him down as he missed a series of putts in the tree to four-foot range. One report claimed that, "'Mack' simply threw away half a dozen strokes and literally presented the title to Smith on a platter."[85] As was the case in some other tournaments, McDermott's putting could, at times, be fragile.

Nevertheless, it was clear that McDermott's game was in good shape but another important factor in his form was the presence of his caddie. Verdant Greene, writing a column in ***The Philadelphia Inquirer,*** claimed that "John Sawyer of Philadelphia............deserves a paragraph all to himself. They constitute a great pair of Jacks to draw to.........He hangs his clothes in Mack's locker" and he acts as "private secretary, caddie, advisor, valet and office boy."[86] This ringing endorsement highlighted the ties that can exist between player and caddie: ties that would be seen to great effect the following month at Brookline, when Francis Ouimet engaged the services of the diminutive Eddie Lowery. And notwithstanding the eventual disappointment at Salisbury, it seemed as if both "Jacks" were in good shape as they headed for the Shawnee Open.

The Shawnee Open of 1913 was significant in a number of ways. The Shawnee course was founded by wealthy New York industrialist, C.C. Worthington who owned a summer residence in the area. Worthington would play an important role in establishing the PGA three years later. And he was responsible for the first advanced gang mower for maintaining golf courses. Prior to this, the job of keeping the fairways in order was often the job of sheep. Worthington hired A.W. Tillinghast to design his course and this was the first in "Tilly's" glittering resume as he would go

84 *The Evening Star*, August 15, 1913.
85 *The Philadelphia Inquirer*, August 15, 1913.
86 *Ibid*, August 24, 1913.

to design Baltusrol, Winged Foot, and Bethpage Black, among many other famous courses. He was also the tournament host and would play an important part in the week's events. What gave the event added spice and publicity was the presence of Harry Vardon and Ted Ray who were playing exhibitions throughout the land and the Shawnee stop was seen as ideal preparation for the upcoming National Open at Brookline the following month. And at this stage, a little controversy surrounding Vardon and Ray arose.

Over many years, the question of appearance money in golf has been a thorny issue. That is to say professional players are paid to appear in tournaments where there is prize money on offer, as opposed to playing in an exhibition match where there is no prize money but where there is an agreed fee before the players tee-off. When it came to light that the two British stars were receiving appearance money for playing at Shawnee, a great deal of criticism came their way, and it was reported on in Britain, as well as in America. On their exhibition tour before and after Shawnee, the players received a combined fee of $350 per stop. At Shawnee it was £200 or a little less than $300. Considering the first prize at Shawnee was $200, Vardon and Ray would have a profitable week regardless of the tournament outcome. When challenged, about the issue it was reported that "both expressed surprise and indignation that their actions should have incensed the American Golf Association...............Vardon and Ray pointed out that they have twice as many offers extended by clubs all over the country as they could accept, and it would be foolish to refuse money that was thrust on them" Ted Ray went so far as to say that he and Vardon worked a lot harder than many vaudeville acts and were entitled to be paid accordingly.[87]

If McDermott objected to appearance money being paid to the two Britons, he did not say so publicly. When the tournament started, there was a very strong field made up of the homebreds like McDermott, the imported pros like Alex Smith, and the British invaders. A very much lesser- known member of the invaders was Wilfrid Reid who was also preparing for Brookline and who in time, would emigrate and forge a fine career as a professional at some of America's top clubs such as Broadmoor and Seminole. He would also become a course designer of some repute. For a time, at least, Reid featured at Brookline

Even at this relatively early stage of the summer and over two months before the U.S. Open, British newspapers were highlighting the challenges that lay ahead

87 *The Sheffield Daily Telegraph*, August 23, 1913.

for the British invaders. For example, ***The Sketch,*** which carried regular golf columns, reported that, "There has been a great change in American golf................in America, Vardon and Ray will have McDermott chiefly to fear. He is clearly a far better player than British golfers believed him to be, attaching far too much importance to his failure to qualify in the Open Championship at Muirfield last year. I have heard an Open champion say that his first nine holes in the third round at Hoylake was the best thing done at the recent meeting there. His driving is beautifully crisp, his iron play sound."[88] McDermott's 36 for the first nine in the third round at Hoylake was indeed golf of the highest order, and even if his challenge faltered a little after that, it was clear that his abilities had not gone un-noticed. And ahead of his departure for America, Harry Vardon gave an interview to England's premier golfing journal, *Golf Illustrated*, in which he too lauded McDermott. *The Brooklyn Daily Eagle*, quoting from the interview, reported that, "Vardon thinks that the Britishers most dangerous rival will be J.J. McDermott................Since his first appearance in this country twelve months ago, Vardon considers that McDermott has improved out of all knowledge and now is a formidable opponent for even the best man Britain can produce."[89]

As it transpired, the claims in ***The Sketch*** and ***Golf Illustrated***, proved to be accurate, certainly at Shawnee, as John McDermott won the tournament in a most convincing manner. As host, Tillinghast paired McDermott and Alex Smith together for the final 36 holes perhaps, given the history between the pair, to add spice to the proceedings. If so, he was not disappointed for, as referee with a front row seat, he recalled that "the two were not neglecting opportunities for quiet banter and badgering, particularly during the play of the late holes of the afternoon."[90] On that final 36 holes, McDermott shot 70-74 and with a score of 293 won by eight from Smith and collected a prize of $200. Vardon finished fifth on 306 and Ray eighth on 308. Reports of what ensued have varied but Tillinghast's account, as a first hand and reliable witness, is compelling. Part of his role as tournament director and club president was to hand the Shawnee Open trophy to this "bumptious youth."

Calling McDermott by such a name referred to an earlier meeting between the two and Tillinghast would describe the incident as follows:

---

88 *The Sketch*, July 13, 1913.
89 *The Brooklyn Daily Eagle*, August 23, 1913.
90 Tillinghast, p 95.

One day, a little fellow came to me and recalled the fact that he had caddied for me on a number of occasions; told me that he had become a pro at a little nine-hole course in Merchantville, in South Jersey, but yearning for better things, asked me to use my influence in getting him the vacancy at well-known Philadelphia Cricket Club. This suggestion, coming from an utterly unknown, rather staggered me by its incongruity, but when I told him that already I had succeeded in placing ex-champion, Willie Anderson, at the Cricket Club, he remarked that it was a great pity as he could beat Anderson for red apples or green money, and further he could beat any pro in the Philadelphia district. This supreme egoism left me quite cold and, frankly, I regarded McDermott merely as a bumptious youth, who needed a good trimming to show him his place." [91]

As well as his talents as a course architect, Tillinghast was also a golf writer and frequently covered golfing matters, notably in the Philadelphia region, where he grew up and played much of his golf. And despite his earlier views on McDermott, a relationship developed between the two men. Indeed, Tillinghast went on to offer some sound advice to the youthful McDermott. "I told him he was hurting himself and in short, advised him to permit his game to talk for him."[92] These wise words were welcomed by McDermott, who told Tillinghast that "the future would find him playing the game and minding his tongue." The senior man's response to this was, "I liked McDermott from that moment, and whenever I visited him at Atlantic City, he was sticking strictly to business."[93] The evidence from Shawnee suggests that, sadly, McDermott did not simply "let his game talk for him." But the exchanges between the pair suggest that a healthy respect grew between them and perhaps explains why Tillinghast, more than most, was understanding of the fall-out from Shawnee.

In this regard, almost three years after the incident, Tillinghast shed a great deal more light on events in Shawnee. In an article, he claimed that "my reason for a long silence may be attributed only to keep alive the incident which should have been killed and buried before it worked evil."[94] Tillinghast went on to describe what happened after the tournament.

as McDermott received his prize money and the gold medal when there were calls for a speech.......................in a moment of confusion without more ado

91 *Ibid*, p 94.

92 *The Public Ledger*, July 2, 1913.

93 *Ibid*.

94 Tillinghast, p 94.

the young pro referred to "What the Little American Boy Could Do" to foreign invaders, (who stood right there) and promised that none need fear that the Open title would go across seas: as he predicted he would give them the same medicine at Brookline. Certainly, this flaunting of extreme optimism in the very face of the invaders, was uncalled for and although all those who heard him could not approve of it, they were mindful of the fact that the comparatively uneducated lad was not a speechmaker, but rather a remarkably fine golfer who possessed in himself a confidence which was developed to an extraordinary degree. It was this supreme confidence which made McDermott the great golfer that he was, and it was the same supreme confidence which prompted him to predict failure in the presence of the British visitors.[95]

As an eye witness to events, Tillinghast's words had to be respected and he went on to recall how, "I stood by McDermott's elbow when he offered an apology to Vardon and Ray, and I am sure that the Britons were satisfied in their own hearts that the lad had spoken thoughtlessly and there the incident would have ended, but the avalanche of publicity which followed soon after was the rat which gnawed the foundation timbers of the greatest golf game ever produced in America. Time enables most men to forget, but McDermott never forgot."[96]

At Tillinghast's request, the "avalanche of publicity" was suppressed for a number of days as most of the writers present respected their host and saw the potential damage that might arise if they wrote about the event. However, as Tillinghast went on to say, there was a "scrivener who determined to turn it to his account and in this way it found publicity. Two days later this fellow broke the story in several papers and the fat was in the fire." It was admirable that despite his previous reservations about McDermott's manners, Tillinghast was generous enough to see the bigger picture and tried to protect the young champion. He even went on to suggest that McDermott be treated with mercy as he was "a golfer - not a speechmaker"[97] But as it transpired, it was to no avail.

The fall-out from the incident was both immediate and lasting. It was reported that "Nothing else was talked about yesterday by the professionals as they scattered on their homeward ways. The homebreds, of whom McDermott is one, if possible being more indignant over the affair than the foreign- born pros. One of

95 Ibid, p 95.
96 Ibid, p 95.
97 Ibid, p 96.

them said to-day: "The cables will be full of the matter within hours and American professionals can be sure of a cool reception abroad for years to come. The word Shawnee will mean the same in England that Concord and Lexington did during the American Revolution."[98] The references to the first two battles in America's fight for independence from the British Empire served only to add fuel to the diplomatic fire that was already burning.

As noted above, in an immediate attempt to repair at least some of the damage, McDermott immediately apologized to Vardon and Ray who according to some accounts accepted. According to Mark Frost's detailed account, the vastly experienced British pros put it down to youthful exuberance from a man who had just won the tournament.[99] However, Frost also recorded that after handshakes all 'round, McDermott shouted "But you are still not going to take the cup back!" This enraged the more combustible Ray who according to Frost had to be tackled by Vardon "to keep him off the kid,"[100] There may have been some truth in this account of Ray's reaction as at the time, a newspaper report was widely circulated which claimed that, "Later McDermott offered an apology to Ray who declined to accept his apology unless made publicly."[101] And the above article from the "scrivener" was very pro Vardon and Ray and highly critical of McDermott. This in turn sparked a flood of criticism for his unsporting conduct and then the USGA became involved.

At this stage it is reasonable to suggest that a certain degree of snobbery and deference became evident. Despite the United States' growing global power and influence, there still existed a certain amount of reverence towards Britain where golf was concerned. It was after all "their game" in that golf began across the Atlantic and at that stage, the most influential figures in the Royal and Ancient game in the U.S. were mostly British immigrants. This was the case in tournament play, teaching, club-making, and course design. In this regard, the U.S. golfing establishment appeared determined to put an immature, raw, ex-caddy in his place for upsetting the established golfing stars from the land where the game originated. If this was the case, there was a certain irony as both Ray and Vardon came from extremely modest backgrounds in Jersey and like McDermott, emerged as champions from the caddy ranks. And both men had to contend with the unquestioned snobbery

---

98 *The Philadelphia Inquirer*, August 25, 1913.

99 M. Frost, *The Greatest Game Ever Played*, (Great Britain: Time Warner Paperbacks, 2003), p. 157.

100 *Ibid*.

101 *The Evening Bulletin*, August 27, 1913.

that existed in Britain as the gentleman amateur was regarded as superior in rank to the more menial professional.

In any event, the U.S. golfing establishment became involved in the controversy with the editor of *Golf* magazine, Max Behr, having his say. In an open letter addressed to VARDON, RAY AND REID, he wrote, "As the editor of this magazine and as one who feels himself in touch with the sentiments of American golfers, I wish in this public manner to express the deep regret and humiliation we all feel for the uncalled-for affront you received at the hands of our Open Champion J.J. McDermott."[102] Behr continued in the same vein and ended by comparing McDermott's outburst at Shawnee as being akin to that of a prize-fighter. Behr was undoubtedly a strong voice in American golf and a man with the right golfing background. A graduate of Yale, and with Scottish ancestry, apart from his writings, he was a losing finalist in the 1908 U.S. Amateur Championship. However, he made a number of assumptions in his comments, notably that he spoke for "all" American golfers, when it is more likely that he spoke for pockets of the golfing establishment. And using the word, "humiliation" because he was "in touch with the sentiments of American golfers," was again somewhat presumptuous. The Shawnee incident was regrettable but hardly cause for the entire American golfing family to feel humiliated.

In addition to Behr, the USGA became formally involved and it was reported that "Officials of the National Association last week asked correspondents of the London Journals to make it clear that the organization disclaimed all responsibility for such remarks and intimated that official censure of McDermott would follow."[103] Furthermore the USGA "have indicated to McDermott in the clearest possible way that such indiscretions as that at Shawnee cannot be tolerated in an aspirant for the championship honours and that unless he can keep a better guard upon the unruly member, they will find themselves unable to accept his entry."[104] At one stage it looked as if the USGA might follow through and deny McDermott the chance to defend his National title- leading the way in all of this was the President of the USGA, Robert Watson.

Watson, again displaying a certain deference towards British golf referred to earlier, was clearly not content to deal with the matter domestically. He followed up on the USGA's earlier edicts to London journalists and, in a personal interview

102 *Golf Illustrated*, UK, September 19, 1913.
103 *The Evening World*, September 8, 1913.
104 *The Sheffield Daily Telegraph*, September 19, 1913.

given to London's *Daily Mail,* he was quoted as follows regarding McDermott, "He will never forget the letter I have written to him and I hope you will make British golfers understand how repugnant to us and how thoroughly unrepresentative of our sentiments such comment is."[105] As it turned out McDermott was allowed to play at Brookline, but there is no doubt that the whole incident and its aftermath, especially the response of the USGA, damaged his spirt and his confidence in the longer term.

The *Daily Mail* article, which was determined to paint McDermott in the worst possible light, also brought his long-time friends, Tom McNamara and Mike Brady, into the proceedings. In an attempt to "divide and conquer," the report added that, "Brady and McNamara the other two foremost homebreds who with the champion, make up the "American Triumvirate" have taken the fullest measures to disassociate themselves from their colleague's attitude, and exhibition matches in which they were to appear have been modified or cancelled."[106] These comments, which were designed to wound McDermott, do not appear to have any basis in fact. As we shall see, McDermott did a series of exhibition matches with Tom McNamara after Brookline and the friendship between the three men remained strong.

The matter of McDermott's outburst at Shawnee and its aftermath, has long been written about by golf's chroniclers. Less space, however, has been given to *why* he behaved in such a fashion. Steve Eubanks has written persuasively that McDermott's behavior may have been the first signs of the schizophrenic condition that would so tragically dog him for much of his life.[107] There may be merit in this view as McDermott's behavior was extreme, and without precedent in the world of top-class professional golf. On a more pragmatic level, however, there may have been other forces at play.

For example, it is possible that McDermott believed that as a double U.S. Open Champion, he was entitled to more respect than he received from Britain and its leading golfers. And that it was this resentment that surfaced at Shawnee. We will recall that in 1912, McDermott competed in The Open Championship at Muirfield and having gone into the championship full of confidence, he failed to qualify after a disastrous first round of 91. While his performance was the subject of some ridicule from the locals, McDermott in any event felt that as a U.S. Open Champion, he was

105 *Golf Illustrated*, UK, September 19, 1913.
106 *Ibid.*
107 Eubanks.

not afforded the respect he deserved. There may have been more than a grain of truth in this as Tillinghast again recorded, when referring to that Open at Muirfield. He wrote that at Shawnee, McDermott "only was repeating something which had been told to him when he first visited Great Britain to play for the British title....... Andrew Kirkaldy the blunt Scotch pro had said to him, "If it's our Open you're after, ye micht be at home, laddie,"[108]

Furthermore, while Vardon may have been diplomatic during his American tour of 1913, he was less so when he returned home. In an article titled "Vardon Amplifies His American Appraisals," *The Seattle Daily Times* reported that "Vardon, however, unqualifiedly said to the writer that Chick Evans was the best golfer in the United States. He apparently did not have McDermott or any other professional in mind at that time. He meant that the Chicago youth was the best, amateur or professional."[109] The article recorded how, on his return home, Vardon gave credit to McDermott but his attitude may have been a sore point with the highly charged American who undoubtedly, for whatever reason, carried a sizeable chip on his shoulder. As we saw, Vardon's views on McDermott appear to have changed between 1913 and 1915, but this may not have been enough for the U.S. Open champion who was clearly a man with a long memory. And, while McDermott's resentment of British attitudes towards him (perceived or otherwise) does not condone his behavior at Shawnee, it may shed some light on why he acted in such a manner.

With all the negative publicity surrounding the incident, it was easy to forget that McDermott played very well at Shawnee. And when writing of the golf played, rather than the controversy that followed, Tillinghast offered some interesting views on McDermott's accuracy, especially with his favored mashie. By this stage he knew McDermott and his background quite well and he suggested that, "While not a proficient pupil in our public schools [he] had mastered calculus before he was 14 years of age, and this bred-in-the-bone faculty of his, together with his supreme confidence, I think is the solution of his success for the last three years in our open championship." And, on his play at Shawnee, Tillinghast continued, "I saw him go ahead 100 and in some instances 150 yards to calculate the distance to the hole and then, with supreme confidence, play the shot to the hole with a precision which is uncanny." Tillinghast concluded his comments by remarking that Vardon

108 Tillinghast, p 96.
109 *The Seattle Daily Times*, December 31, 1913.

and Ray agreed that "his calculation of distances surpassed anything which they have ever seen."[110] Tillinghast was a highly respected figure, and if his views are to be taken seriously, it would seem that long before Deane Beman and Jack Nicklaus popularized measuring off distances, notably in the early 1960's, John McDermott had devised his own way of minimizing the margin for error when playing approach shots.

Despite the excellence of his play at Shawnee, however, some saw McDermott's victory as irrelevant in terms of what might happen at Brookline with one writer suggesting that "the result should not be taken seriously by any close followers of golf in this country." The journalist then condescendingly reported that the tournament was "run as a sort of advertisement for the hotel links upon which it was played."[111] However, one English writer saw it as important in terms of what might happen at the upcoming U.S. Open. Henry Leach was a very prominent and respected British writer/journalist and after Shawnee he wrote, "So here we have McDermott thirteen strokes better than Harry Vardon and fifteen better than Ray. Of course, it may well work out very differently at Brookline. The test will be better and our men will be much better acclimatized. But the Shawnee business makes me and other British golfers out here uneasy. If McDermott wins this championship we shall never hear the end of it. I cannot help thinking that our men have made a mistake in playing in tournaments of this kind before the championship. They had nothing to gain by doing so- except a few dollars- and very much to lose."[112] Leach's article was one of many in the British newspapers in advance of Brookline and a consistent nationalist theme emerged through phrases like "our men," and "we shall never hear the end of it."

On the other hand, however, The United States also showed its true colors after Shawnee and one newspaper heralded the fact that "For the first time in the history of the game an American-born and an American-bred player beat the best of Britain's golfers................It was no hollow victory either, but a crushing, smashing defeat that will take the glory out of Vardon and Ray's playing." And, in a nod towards the exhibition fees being received by the British pair, the piece continued," McDermott showed to-day that we have the "goods" right here in this

110 *The Philadelphia Record*, August 31, 1913.
111 *The Daily News And Leader*, August 26, 1913.
112 *The Sketch*, September 17, 1913.

country, without the need for any importation."[113] Strong words such a "crushing" and "smashing" left nothing to the imagination. Ahead of the U.S. Open, it was very much a question of Britain versus America in the quest for golfing supremacy.

The 1913 U.S. Open at the Country Club Brookline, was given advance billing as "what will prove to be the greatest open golf championship in the history of the United States."[114] This lofty claim was in part due to the arrival of international stars such as the France's Louis Tellier. However, what gave the Championship its imprimatur then and for evermore, was the presence of the British invaders, "Vardon and Ray past winners of the open championship of Great Britain which is in reality a world's championship."[115] American reverence for these two golfing giants ***and*** for the Open Championship, was there for all to see. And even from a distance of over a century, it remains, perhaps, the most celebrated championship in the rich history of golf in America. It even entered popular culture when it became the only National Open (to date) that has attracted the attention of Hollywood with a movie based on (and with the same title as) Mark Frost's seminal book, *The Greatest Game Ever Played*.

As noted at the start of this book, the 1913 U.S. Open was seen as a turning point in American golf history with the unknown amateur caddie, Francis Ouimet, beating Vardon and Ray. And the movie fully conveys the momentous achievements of Ouimet at Brookline. But if Ouimet is cast on screen as its hero, then John McDermott is deliberately cast as the pantomime villain. With more than a slice of poetic license, the unfortunate scenes from Shawnee are transplanted to Brookline and here we see actor Michael Weaver, as John McDermott, in full voice as he warns Ray and Vardon that the trophy is not going back across the Atlantic. And in case anyone would forget McDermott's Irish heritage, Weaver has a fine head of reddish hair complete with matching moustache. The image of the feisty, red-headed Irishman, is complete.

The details of the Championship itself have been well documented with the local caddie, Ouimet, defeating Vardon and Ray in an 18- hole play- off and so securing his rightful place in American golfing lore. What featured far less prominently was, that despite the fall-out from Shawnee, John McDermott put up a very creditable defense of his title. In the 36-hole qualifying rounds, he shot 81 and 80 which were

---

113 *The Brooklyn Daily Eagle*, August 29, 1913.
114 *The Boston Sunday Post*, September 14, 1913.
115 *Ibid*.

modest but comfortably inside the required mark of 166. Ray led the field on 148, with Vardon and Reid completing the top three qualifiers. And even before the Championship proper started, one British newspaper could not contain its pleasure regarding McDermott's modest showing. It began, "The three British competitors have therefore topped the list- a fact which will probably have left McDermott's optimism tottering on its base."

And, it continued, "McDermott being the man from whom most was feared, will have, in Yankee language, to serve out a better class of goods if the championship is to be retained in the States."[116] Actually, the holder did produce some "top class goods" as he began the championship with a run of 4-3-4-4-3-4-3 and it looked as if he might continue his form from the previous three U.S. Opens. However, McDermott did drop back after that blistering start but his first round of 74 left him well placed and only three shots back of Alex Ross and MacDonald Smith. That, however, was as good as it got for McDermott, nevertheless he fought all the way and his total of 308 left him only four strokes out of a play-off. Taking everything into account, it was a noble defense of his title.

There is no doubt that Ouimet's victory was a popular one but even before the play-off had been decided, there was, again, more than a degree of pleasure seen in Britain at McDermott's failure to retain his crown. One "On The Links" column read,

> The low position taken by McDermott in the present championship will hardly cause any regret either in England or America..................McDermott has had to eat his words completely. He said that the Englishmen hadn't a Chinaman's chance of winning the championship and that they might as well go home without playing for it. We have nothing to say against McDermott's golf........... but we are glad that retribution has followed fast on his indiscreet outburst...... he has found out that men like Vardon and Ray are still his masters at the Royal and Ancient game.[117]

Such displays of jingoism and schadenfreude would not have been uncommon in the media but in this case the report was inaccurate. First of all, McDermott's finish of only four shots behind the winning total was not in any way "lowly." And second, Vardon and Ray may have remained the "masters" but at Brookline they were well beaten in the play-off by the relatively unknown American, Francis

---

116 *The Globe*, September 19, 1913.
117 *The Star Green 'Un*, September 20, 1913.

Ouimet. And much later, Ouimet, with the grace that was the hallmark of his career, remembered the role McDermott played in his victory. He recalled, "Just before I started for the first tee, John McDermott, then the ex-champion, came to me and said, 'Francis, play your own game. Don't watch them at all.' I honestly think that those words did more to bring victory my way than anything else. I had the honor and drove a good ball down the middle of the course."[118] McDermott must have been bitterly disappointed not to be the man who beat Ray and Vardon, and according to Mark Frost's vivid account of proceedings, at the end of 72 holes, he stood before the gallery, "exhausted, scarred and pale, looking around darkly at the crowd surrounding the green. It was impossible to tell: Did he see friends or enemies?"[119] Frost's account of McDermott's demeanor conveys the image of a man whose mental state was in turmoil. Regardless, however, of any inner demons he may have been fighting, McDermott was generous and patriotic enough to stay over an extra day and do all he could to help keep the trophy in America.

The play-off took place on September 20 and that evening an article appeared in *The Evening World* in which Harry Vardon made a diplomatic reference to John McDermott. The piece, appearing within hours of the finish was largely about Ouimet's triumph. And Vardon was honest enough to admit that he had neither heard of nor seen the young amateur before the previous day. Of McDermott he had this to say, "We were favorably impressed with John J. .McDermott, national open champion, in England, and came over expecting a stiff fight from him. He lived up to our expectations when, after a disappointing first day, he rallied nobly and finished with 308.[120] Vardon's comments, however gracious they may appear, should be qualified to a certain degree. First of all, the article was clearly ghost written and presumably another well-earned source of income for the world's most famous player. Second, as the article was for American consumption, it would have been remiss if no mention was made of America's leading player. And third, as we saw, Vardon's views, when he was back on home soil, struck a slightly different note.

A supporting player at Brookline was a 20- year-old Walter Hagen from Rochester who was making his National Open debut. Hagen had a wonderful championship finishing only three shots behind Ouimet, Vardon and Ray. Even at this early stage, Hagen displayed the self-confidence that would mark his career.

118 *The Philadelphia Inquirer*, July 23, 1916.,
119 Frost, p 331.
120 *The Evening World*, September 20, 1913.

On seeing McDermott in the locker room before the championship he said, "You're Johnny McDermott aren't you? Well, I'm glad to know you. I'm W.C. Hagen from Rochester and I've come over to help you boys take care of Vardon and Ray." And, Hagen later recalled that this "brassy introduction brought chuckles from the experienced professionals who overheard him."[121] Hagen may have had a great deal more charm than John McDermott, and even though he was unproven at this stage, he too liked to feel respected. At Brookline he felt that the reaction in the locker room to his brashness was discourteous. And, using this perceived slight as a motivational tool, he vowed to show them all next year by winning the National Open. This he did at the Midlothian Club, Illinois, and so began one of the most successful and colorful careers in golf. Hagen had played at Shawnee and perhaps his "take care of Vardon and Ray" remark was a show of support for Mc Dermott after the fallout that had occurred. In any event, W.C. Hagen from Rochester would, in later years, be a very good friend to John McDermott.

The general consensus among golf commentators and historians is that John McDermott's career went into a tailspin after events at Shawnee. Indeed, his supporter, Tillinghast, claimed that at Brookline "he played like a dead man. His indifferent performance was so far below his normal game that it showed how terribly his mind was upset. There was absolutely no life, there was no sting to his shots- then or ever again."[122] The facts about McDeremott's form suggest otherwise, as finishing only four shots out of a play-off at The Country Club was not that far "below his normal game" and certainly not the golf of a "dead man." Even Grantland Rice, who was a great champion of McDermott, shared Tillinghast's views and much later recalled how, "in 1913, at Shawnee, with one of the greatest fields on record, he not only led the parade, but finished thirteen strokes beyond Harry Vardon. That was John McDermott's last stand in American golf. The career that started brilliantly in 1910, went up in smoke after the Shawnee tournament and from that point on, McDermott faded out of public golfing life, broken mentally and physically."[123] However, while this period may have been the start of McDermott's decline, it was gradual. The showing at Brookline was more than creditable and the following week, he played an exhibition at the Bethlehem Club in the company of Brady and McNamara. This Irish-American trio was very much in demand for

---

121 S. R. Lowe, *Sir Walter and Mr. Jones*, (Chelsea, MI, Sleeping Bear Press, 2000), p. 26.
122 Tillinghast, p. 96.
123 *The Indianapolis Star*, March 7, 1920.

such matches. Here McDermott broke the course record with a two-under round of 71. And then, the following month he embarked on a week-long exhibition tour, again in the company of Tom McNamara. This hardly suggested the mentality of a man who had been severely scarred by recent events. The exhibition tour, as well as being lucrative, was also ideal preparation for the Western Open in Memphis starting on October 15.

At this time, there were only two professional major championships in the golfing calendar- the Open and the U.S. Open. The PGA did not begin until 1916 and the Masters had its first outing in 1934. And, both before and for long after 1913, the Western Open was the second ranked tournament in the United States. Much of this prestige was due to two factors: first, it began in 1899 (the second oldest to the U.S. Open), and second, the quality of the fields the tournament attracted and its roll of honor. For example, the first man to win the National Open four times, Willie Anderson, was also a four- time winner of the Western Open. Anderson, another transplanted Scot, came from the golfing heartland of North Berwick. And the defending champion in 1913 was another Scotsman, this time MacDonald Smith from Carnoustie who, despite many tournament victories, would go down in history as one of the best men never to win a major.

The Western Open that year was played at the Memphis Country Club and here John McDermott put his name on the tournament's illustrious roll of honor with a comprehensive victory. Playing, often in wet conditions, he again demonstrated his class. After three rounds, he led by four from Mike Brady and closed out the tournament with a 75 and a seven- shot victory over Brady. His one under par score of 295 was the third lowest total in the history of the championship and his winning purse was $300. And, the Western Open was another "first" for McDermott as up to then, no home-born pro had won the title. So, just a few short weeks after Brookline, John McDermott had won the second most prized domestic trophy in American professional golf. There was clearly some "sting" left in his shots at Memphis. One footnote to the Western Open. McDermott's first prize of $300 was sizeable for that era. However, after him only the players down as far as Tom McNamara in fifth place, ($50), collected any cash. For the other 26 professionals who completed 72 holes there was nothing. Such was the lot of the pros at that time and a compelling reason why a good club position was so important.

The remainder of 1913 brought mixed news for John McDermott. There was little tournament play on offer but there were rumors that he may be in line for the prestigious club professional's job at Baltusrol. But reports did consistently emerge in November on McDermott's mental health - and even Harry Vardon saw fit, before his departure, to refer to it sympathetically. For a time, it seemed as if there was to be a chance for McDermott (with Tom McNamara) to compete against Vardon and Ray on November 8, just before the pair left for Britain. A challenge match was arranged with the two "Macks" taking on the British pair at McDermott's home club of Atlantic City. It looked like a tantalising prospect. The game was the last stop of the Vardon and Ray nationwide tour that had so captivated American golf fans and had seen them lose only one of these contests. As it transpired, Vardon and Ray wired McDermott to call off the match, "for no apparent reason."[124] In any event, by the scheduled date of November 8, news of McDermott's health had broken to which Vardon made reference to this before boarding his ship. He was quoted as diplomatically saying that he believed McDermott's best days were ahead of him and that "he was glad that McDermott's breakdown has proved to be nothing worse than a cold and a neuralgic headache and that he went to his mother's home for rest rather than a sanitarium for treatment."[125] Sadly the prognosis for McDermott was far worse than the information provided to Vardon.

Then, there were stories that earlier in the year, he had lost heavily on ill-advised investments and there was the incident at Shawnee with the resultant adverse publicity. Speculation grew that all of these factors combined, contributed to a deterioration in the golfer's mental health. Reports from the time abounded with news of his condition, and on the days of November first and second 1913, the newspapers, nationally, were full of stories about John McDermott and his well-being, with one more extreme headline referring to him as a "nervous wreck." In general, however, the reports were more moderate as evidenced by ***The Boston Evening Transcript.*** Here a headline on November 1st ran with "Former Golf Champion Has A Breakdown." And, it went on to report that

> He turned dangerously ill at midnight last night and his parents removed the popular golfer to a private hospital in Philadelphia. McDermott has had a strenuous season, and he has finally succumbed to the strains he has undergone. He practiced consistently one month prior to the invasion abroad last spring and across the water worked under a heavy nervous tension. He returned to America for a string of competitions and again this fall went away

124 *The Evening Star*, October 30, 1913.
125 *The Brooklyn Daily Eagle*, November 14, 1913.

for a fortnight's golfing itinerary. He travelled south and recently annexed the Western championship crown for his long list of honors.[126]

This report was different from many others in that it focused on McDermott's golf, rather than Shawnee or bad investments, as being responsible for his breakdown. At this stage, McDermott was but 22 years old and arguably in his peak years, both physically and mentally, for withstanding the rigors of championship golf. However, the suggestion that the strain of travel, practice, and tournament golf, contributed to his breakdown, cannot be lightly dismissed, especially in such a highly strung individual.

Further evidence of his condition came when it was reported that he failed to "put in an appearance at the Atlantic City Country Club where a golf tournament is being played."[127] The tournament in question was a series of match-play events consisting of different flights with the main prize being the Governor's Cup. And as resident professional, McDermott, was expected to play. Indeed, as host, the two-time National Open Champion would have been the major attraction at an event that was as much a social gathering as it was a golf tournament. His absence suggests that his condition must have been very poor at this time. The trophy was won by prominent New York amateur, and 1911 U.S. Amateur runner-up, Fred Herreshoff. In early December, however, a further report suggested that "McDermott is no longer ill and several weeks ago resumed his duties as professional for the Country Club of Atlantic City"..................and that he is "so much improved that he plans a trip through the South with Michael J. Brady."[128] This contrasting second report may have been an attempt to achieve what today is called "managing the story," and an exhibition tour to resorts like Pinehurst would have been both lucrative and rehabilitating. However, as we shall see later, McDermott was not well enough to make the trip South in early 1914. And, there is little doubt that around this time, the early seeds were sown of the mental illness that would haunt John McDermott for the remainder of his life.

---

126 *The Boston Evening Transcript*, November 1, 1913.

127 *The Cleveland Plain Dealer*, November 2, 1913.

128 *The Perth Amboy News*, December 19, 1913.

# Chapter Six
# 1914 AND AFTER

Even for a two-time U.S. Open champion, the potential for off course earnings was small. Golf lessons and club-making were generally all that was available. However, there was the occasional exception and one of these came John McDermott's way in early 1914. Under a snappy heading of "Tee Up! Smoke Up!", he endorsed Tuxedo tobacco. "Pipe smoking gives added pleasure when the pipe is filled with Tuxedo. Tuxedo provides more keen enjoyment than any other tobacco I know"[129] were the words attributed to McDermott. The brand sold for ten cents a tin and five for a "convenient" pouch. It is interesting that McDermott's words finished with "any other tobacco I know" as from an early age, he was a both a non-drinker and smoker. Perhaps his non-smoking only applied to cigarettes and not tobacco but in any event, he would not have been the only golfer to endorse a product he did not use. Hopefully this rare commercial opportunity earned him a few dollars.

Back in the on-course world, the planned exhibitions in February 1914 took place, but not with John McDermott. Instead, it was reported that he was "forced to give up his annual trip through the South this year......he intended to become one of the party that Tom McNamara is conducting through the South but has decided he is still too poor to make it advisable for him to go.........the best thing he can do is to rest until he has full recovered."[130] Mike Brady accompanied McNamara to play exhibitions in Pinehurst and other popular southern resorts as far down as Florida. And there were even unconfirmed reports that McDermott was injured in a serious car accident. However other accounts of McDermott competing at the Augusta Country Club on February 18 suggest he made some form of recovery. It was here he played in a pro-am with his partner C.B. Speers and McDermott showed his class when shooting a 72, having just come off a train journey to Atlanta. Then, in March, he competed in the North and South tournament at Pinehurst.

129 *The Pittsburgh Press*, January 30, 1914.
130 *The Newark Evening Star*, February 16, 1914.

After the National Open and the Western, the North and South could match any other tournament's standing during this era. The Pinehurst resort was founded and owned by the Tuft family who were also responsible for staging the tournament. The event always attracted a strong field and the fact that it was played over the famed Donal Ross-designed no 2- course, gave it additional prestige. To this day, the Ross masterpiece is generally regarded as one of America's finest courses and it has held many majors including both the Men's and Women's U.S. Open. For a time, it looked as if the Gilbert Nicholls/John McDermott rivalry, originating from 1910, would be rekindled at Pinehurst in 1914. As it turned out, the 36-hole North and South was won by the Englishman with a winning score of 145 and a first prize of $100. John McDermott played creditably and finished just two shots back. In fact, McDermott played himself out of the tournament with is his front nine of 41 in the second 18. However, he fought back with a remarkable back nine of 31 on the no 2 course, and earned $50 for second place.

In addition, around this time, McDermott also announced that he hoped to play in the Open Championship at Prestwick. "McDermott To Try His Luck Abroad" ran one banner- enduring proof that the two-time National Open Champion was still headline news.[131] Notwithstanding the mental problems he undoubtedly had, declaring his intention to play in the Open, alongside his performance at Pinehurst, suggest that McDermott's confidence at this time, was reasonably high. However, during his tour of The South, it was also noted that while he was in good golfing form, "his recent illness has caused him to lose about ten pounds in weight."[132] Considering that McDermott was already of a slight build, this was a worrying sign for a professional athlete with a planned tough schedule ahead of him.

As previously noted, in the absence of a tournament, exhibition matches could be a reliable source of income for top professionals at this time. And, despite his personal problems and some adverse publicity, as two-time National Open Champion, John McDermott was still in demand for such events. One such opportunity presented itself in May 1914 in his home state of Pennsylvania. This was a 36-hole medal play contest at the Whitemarsh Country Club and apart from McDermott, the day also featured Jim Barnes, Louis Tellier and Ben Sayers. McDermott knew Sayers from a match he played with him prior to his first tilt at the Open in Muirfield two years previously. He also knew Tellier who finished fourth at

131 *Duluth News Tribune*, March 25, 1914.
132 *The Ottawa Citizen*, March 20, 1914.

Brookline the previous year and who was part of the French team that decisively defeated an American team after the 1913 Open at Hoylake. At this stage, Barnes was just embarking on one of the most successful careers in professional golf. Originally from Cornwall, England, he was invariably described in the newspapers as "Long Jim Barnes" because of his height. At six feet four, he was a very different physical specimen to John McDermott. Barnes' first of many victories would come in the 1914 Western Open later that year and to-date, he, Tommy Armour and Rory McIlroy are the only British-born professionals to win three of golf's majors- the Open, the PGA and the U.S. Open. Barnes had recently moved to the Whitemarsh Club from Spokane and prior to the event it was reported that "There will be a big slice of money for the low man, while the others will receive something for their day's work."[133] Perhaps it was local knowledge but Barnes won the event with a two-round score of 159 with Sayers on 161 and Tellier on 162. McDermott was a distant fourth on 166.

The appearance of Ben Sayers at Whitemarsh was part of a trip he made to visit his son George, who was pro at the prestigious Merion Club. This was another example of the British imports, who dominated professional golf in America during this era, securing the best club jobs in the land. McDermott and Sayers had time for nine holes at Merion during this visit and the question of the Open Championship at Prestwick that year featured over lunch. Sayers, an admirer of McDermott's, was very keen that the American made the trip but McDermott explained that he was still not sure whether he would travel. He further explained that he would have to pay his own expenses which were sizeable. Considering that on his previous two visits, McDermott's trips across the Atlantic were financed, in part at least, by backers, it seems reasonable to assume that the lack of support in 1914 owed something to his declining form and health. These doubts expressed by McDermott's were confirmed in June by his friend, J.G. Anderson, in an article that appeared in Britain's *Golf Illustrated*. The title of the piece was "McDermott Not Coming Over." Anderson explained, "His reasons are quite sound. He isn't playing well and feels that he could not get into good trim for the open event.....in a big professional match just finished, McDermott and Nicholls were defeated by McDonald Smith and Jock Hutchinson by 2 up and 1 to play. In this play, the former Champion displayed the poorest form he has shown in a number of years and his decision to remain at home is a wise one."[134] But in the event, he decided that he would travel after all.

---

133 *The Seattle Times*, May 10, 1914.
134 *Golf Illustrated* UK, June 5, 1914.

The Open Championship of 1914 at Prestwick, on Scotland's west coast, was memorable for any number of reasons. It was where the first title was played for- it was Harry Vardon's sixth and final victory- it was the last Open for the Great Triumvirate of Vardon, Braid and Taylor- and because of the impending Great War, there would not be another Championship for six years. For the record Vardon beat his friend and rival, Taylor, by three shots with a score of 306. For John McDermott, this Open Championship was memorable for all the wrong reasons. He had announced some months earlier that he intended to compete which may have been a sign of optimism. However, McDermott never made it to the first hole of qualifying due to a series of unfortunate events. Accounts of how this happened vary somewhat with some reports suggesting he mistook the starting date. Another recorded that he was in London "strolling through the West End" when he saw a newspaper with reports of the first day's play at Prestwick. He then travelled through the night and arrived at Prestwick the next morning. [135]

Whatever the reasons, he was late for his tee time. At the time there were suggestions that officials might find a way to allow him to play, but McDermott was having none of it. "I am entirely to blame," he said "it was my own fault. I shall not ask any favor. I do not want to play now, but I shall wait to see the championship played out."[136] If the British Press had sometimes been unkind to McDermott in the past, his sporting manner on this occasion, saw support for his cause. For example, *The Manchester Courier* wrote "It is felt some exception ought to be taken in the highest interests of British sportsmanship in our relations with the American Continent."[137] But McDermott insisted that making an exception, despite the distance he had travelled, would not be fair to his fellow competitors.

However, worse was to follow. McDermott sailed for home on June 17 aboard the Kaiser Willem II, when in a dense fog, the ship collided with a British grain carrier in the English Channel. It was reported that McDermott was having a haircut when the collision happened but he managed to climb on to a lifeboat where he spent 20 hours before being rescued. It can only be imagined what this near- death experience did to his already fragile mind. His sister Gertrude said of the incident, "It was like the last straw. Everything had hit him within a year and it was all bad."[138]

135 *The London Daily News*, June 13, 1914.
136 *The Daily Mirror*, June 13, 1914.
137 *The Manchester Courier*, June 13, 1914.
138 Glenn.

The "everything" to which his sister referred included the episode at Shawnee with Vardon and Ray and the resultant publicity- the rebuke from the USGA- the losses on his investments- his poor mental health- and finally the incident in the English Channel.

After Prestwick and the horrors of his experience in the English Channel, McDermott returned home but his whereabouts were deemed something of a mystery. The newspapers, however, contained many stories about whether or not he would compete in the prestigious Metropolitan Open at Scarsdale in early August. This, it was argued, would be a barometer of his mental and physical well-being. As it happened, McDermott did not compete and MacDonald Smith won with a score of 278 which at that time was the lowest ever total recorded for a professional tournament. However, McDermott did feel well enough to contest the U.S. Open starting August 20 at the Midlothian Club, Chicago, Illinois. This would be a very different Championship to the previous year at Brookline, largely due to the absence of Vardon and Ray and the much-reported transatlantic battle for golfing supremacy. Nevertheless, there was a very strong field present with many former champions playing, including McDermott and of course, the holder, Francis Ouimet.

Ahead of Midlothian, one newspaper at least, struck an optimistic tone regarding McDermott's chances. *The New York Tribune* suggested that "Mack is a power on the links and is not to be overlooked. His misfortunes of the last year or so are not to be taken into consideration. He is a new McDermott, much subdued, yet just as able."[139] However, just as he predicted at Brookline, the young Walter Hagen won the Championship by one from amateur Chick Evans with a score of 290. John McDermott began poorly with a 77 that left him nine shots behind Hagen's 68 and effectively out of contention. However, after that he did not fare too badly as he finished joint ninth on 300. It was at least a respectable showing, even if the claim that he was "just as able" proved not to be the case. For his efforts, he won $50 and this was John McDermott's last appearance in the U.S. Open. He was 23.

After the U.S. Open of 1914, the next important championship on the tournament calendar was the Western Open at Interlachen, Minnesota, to be held during the final week of August. Given that he was reigning champion, and that he had played in the recent U.S. Open, McDermott might have been expected to appear. Again, however, he felt unable to make the trip and defend his title.

139 *The New York Tribune*, September 8, 1914.

Jim Barnes added to his growing reputation by winning the championship. After this, reports on John McDermott became a little sketchy, but his name did surface from time to time. However, one report from November, suggested "McDermott is playing a good game now, although he had a nervous breakdown this summer."[140] And there were reports that he planned an exhibition tour of the north-west in early 1915 with Gilbert Nicholls. However, one report left nobody in doubt as to the true state of McDermott's health. In an article on nerves and golf, *The Seattle Daily Times* used John McDermott as a test case. "How this measure of 'nerves' enters into golf is exemplified in the present condition of John J. McDermott, twice open champion of the United States."

The article then went on to record how McDermott had resigned his position at the Atlantic City Club and continued, "Falling off in his play the past several months has completely demoralised McDermott and made a sick man of him. Sick in a nervous sense but even affecting his physical appearance. Worriment over this phase of his condition caused the pro to first abandon clubmaking, and he gradually passed the instruction work up to his assistants. The resignation as professional in charge came as a climax to his actions. Friends have advised him to remain away from work for at least a year."[141] And a further report confirmed the seriousness of the situation. According to ***The Evening Star***, "Friends say McDermott will quit the game for a while until he had had the opportunity to rest and fit his physical condition thoroughly for the game and his resignation has been looked for some time by local players."[142]

These detailed accounts portray the torment John McDermott was experiencing at this stage of his life. He had not known nor wanted anything but golf since he was a boy caddie. As well as reaching the pinnacle of competitive American golf, he was also in great demand as an instructor and clubmaker, and the Atlantic City Club provided the ideal base from which he could excel in both arts. For him to abandon these parts of his career so dramatically can only be seen as the acts of a desperate man who was in need of help. Help did arrive as, early in 1915, after reports of his "disappearance," he did spend a few weeks in a sanitarium. These dispatches were quickly followed, in February, by suggestions that his health was improving. Even so, golf was out of the question and his planned exhibition tour to Portland and other venues on the Pacific Coast took place with Mike Brady partnering Gilbert Nicholls.

---

140 *The Oregonian*, November 15, 1914.
141 *The Seattle Daily Times*, December 21, 1914.
142 *The Evening Star*, December 5, 1914.

At this point, early in 1915, Grantland Rice, who we know was a great admirer of McDermott's, wrote a telling piece outlining his achievements but also sadly suggesting that his best days were behind him. And, as he often did, Rice finished his comments with some apposite verse.

Today you rule the world beyond denying
Today you hold the height with nerve and skill
To the cheer rings out, each far wind crying
Renown that passing time can never spill
Today you hold the height- but by tomorrow
With sudden slip along the slanting grade
Alone with haunting memories and sorrow,
They do not even know the game you played.[143]

Even at this early stage of John McDermott's career, these beautiful but poignant words vividly captured what had already happened and what lay ahead in the life of the two-time U.S. Open champion. John McDermott certainly ruled the American golfing world for a few glorious years, but as Herbert Warren Wind reminded us earlier, four years after his first major win, people had to "ponder" before they could recall his name.

McDermott did not heed his friend's advice to stay away from golf for a year. He did not enter that year's U.S. Open at Baltusrol, which was won by amateur Jerry Travers who defeated McDermott's friend and perennial bridesmaid, Tom McNamara, by one shot. Along with the foreign professionals, Travers was one part of the twin forces that Grantland Rice referred to when lauding John McDermott for standing up for the homebred professionals. However, a few weeks later, on July 9, 1915, McDermott entered for the Metropolitan Open. His comeback made for a great story and the newspapers played up his re-appearance with great enthusiasm. For example, his local newspaper, *The Philadelphia Inquirer,* spoke for many as it welcomed his return. The aptly named, "Joe Bunker" wrote that "The entrance of Jack McDermott into golf is a great pleasure for the thousands of Philadelphia friends. McDermott is the one great golfer that was developed here and in many ways is the most remarkable golf has ever seen."

143 *The Boston Globe*, February 9, 1915.

Having noted his absence from golf due to his breakdown, the writer reported that "his friends hope his recovery is permanent." Joe Bunker, however, did go on to say that "McDermott has had one great fault and that has been his antipathy to everything foreign"[144] It seemed that even while lavishing excessive praise and good wishes on the local hero, the ghosts of Shawnee and Brookline were never far away. And, in this regard, Bunker's final comments were unfair as McDermott, on three occasions, made the long journey to Britain to contest The Open Championship. He also competed in France on two occasions. These were hardly the actions of man who was anti "everything foreign."

The Metropolitan Open of 1915 was held at the Fox Hills Club on Staten Island and at that time was reputed to have the largest clubhouse in the land. Fox Hills was both host and sponsor of the Metropolitan Open. McDermott started remarkably well in very wet conditions, and after two rounds of 71 and 75, he lay just one shot behind Walter Hagen and Robert MacDonald. As was the case before the tournament began, the newspapers were full of support for the former champion's first 36 holes. One report began, "It was a display of nerve and gameness rarely seen in any sport. Both spectators and players paid the little fellow a remarkable tribute for his feat in coming almost direct from a sanitarium to compete against some of the greatest gofers ever gathered."[145] After that, however, mental and physical fatigue caught up with McDermott and two closing rounds of 78 and 81 saw him finish out of the money on 305, 13 shots behind Gilbert Nicholls and Robert MacDonald who tied on 292. Nicholls won the play-off.

Whether or not McDermott's re-entry into tournament golf was ill judged is open to debate but it was short lived, and it was against the advice of his friends. It was also contrary to the wishes of his doctors and it was later reported that McDermott "was under a physician's eye after each round at Fox Hills." This account further reported that McDermott "has had a surprising number of pupils of doctors the country over, many of whom have taken an extraordinary interest in him personally. The other day one of them said he thought that there was no doubt that if McDermott had the patience to continue rest cure until next spring, he would, within a couple of seasons, regain his old supremacy."[146] Allowances should be made for the anecdotal nature of this report, especially in regard to McDermott's ability

144 *The Philadelphia Inquirer*, July 12, 1915.
145 *The Evening World*, July 9, 1915.
146 *The Philadelphia Inquirer*, July 25, 1915.

to "regain his old supremacy." However, there seems little doubt that as well as receiving wide public support during his comeback, McDermott was also receiving a great degree of medical advice that was surely in his best interests.

Later that month, McDermott was supposed to play the New Hampshire tournament but instead he phoned some friends to say that, accompanied by his sister, he was going for some recuperation to the scenic White Mountains area in Bethlehem, New Hampshire. But he remained spirited and "stated that he knew full well that he was on the high road to complete recovery and that in the Fall he would be in the thick of the fight again."[147] It would seem, however, that his break from the game and his recuperation, did not exclude all forms of golf as there was a report that in the company of Mr LeRoy, he played some "remarkable" golf at the Bethlehem Club.[148] Again, however, and perhaps mirroring McDermott's confused state of mind, a month later another, and a very different report, appeared. This claimed that McDermott "has played in his last championship tourney..........[he] will leave in a few days for Boston where he will take up residence."[149] The Boston trip did not materialize.

Around this time, approaching the Fall of 1915, fewer accounts of John McDermott appeared in the newspapers. There were a limited number of tournaments on offer at this time of year and in any event, he had retired, either officially or unofficially. The following year, 1916, followed much the same path but sadly, accounts of his poor health and circumstances began to appear, not with great regularity, but often enough to be noticed. For example, *The Pittsburgh Post Gazette* began one report on his condition in somewhat philosophical mode. "John J. McDermott." It began, "the greatest golfer ever developed in America is now in an asylum. The paths of glory do not always lead to rosebuds of rest." However, it then concluded in a less understanding fashion with, "McDermott, when the break came had too far to fall to stand the crash. So, it left him wrecked and broken where he is to-day." [150]

Then, *The New Brunswick Daily Times* of April 10 ran a headline- "Jack McDermott Is Lost Forever As A Golfer." However, in a more compassionate manner than *The Pittsburgh Post Gazette*, it went on to report how "Last year he went to the Brae

147 *The Springfield Daily News*, July 14, 1915.
148 *The New York Daily Tribune*, July 25, 1915.
149 *The Harrisburg Telegraph*, August 31, 1915.
150 *The Pittsburgh Post Gazette*, April 9, 1916.

Burn private sanitarium at Primrose PA, and the stay there seemed to do him good. Last November it was announced that he had gone to Boston to enter business but instead he went to hospital. He has no funds and is now absolutely dependent upon his friends. Contributions of any sum may be sent to Harrison Townsend of 1000 Chestnut Street Philadelphia. McDermott is a member of The Knights of Columbus and has many friends among the members of the New Brunswick Council." The article ended with, "Mr Townsend hopes that Mac's many friends will help the youngster who can no longer help himself."[151] Apart from his connections to The Knights of Columbus, Townsend was, for many years, secretary/treasurer of the Philadelphia Golf Association, and, in this role, as we know, was instrumental in funding the golfer's trip to Muirfield for the 1912 Open Championship. He was an influential figure in terms of finding support for John McDermott during this period.

This honest, if sad account, of McDermott's circumstances, highlights some issues. For instance, how was it that he had "no funds." Admittedly, tournament wining's in this era were not substantial but with victories, such as the U.S. Open, many doors opened. And as we saw, John McDermott was in demand for exhibitions, lessons, and club design. He was also known as someone who successfully played "money matches" over the years. And he did not drink or smoke. Perhaps the private sanitarium at Brae Burn soaked up his earnings and he was left with little after that. If this was the case, it was no major surprise that the Knights of Columbus offered help. The organization, founded in 1882, was for practicing male Catholics and it acted largely as a benevolent society for working class and immigrant communities. As we know. before his more recent problems, McDermott had attended meetings of "The Knights." As noted earlier his immigrant, Catholic/Irish roots, were important to him and so, it was no real surprise that he gravitated towards the organization. This would not be the last time requests were made to help John McDermott.

Finally, there came official and conclusive proof both of McDermott's mental health and his financial circumstances. Under the heading, "In The Matter Of John McDermott, A LUNATIC- And now to wit: June 23rd 1916, the Court Orders and decrees that the within-named John J. McDermott be taken to the State Hospital for the Insane at Norristown PA, and be detained and supported there at the expense of the City and County of Philadelphia so long as he continues of unsound mind or until he is thence discharged by due process of law." The order went on to state that

151 *The New Brunswick Daily Times*, April 10, 1916.

his mother, Margaret, should pay the city $1.75 per week for the support of the, "said lunatic."[152]

Norristown was very much part of local history as the land originally belonged to the founding father of Pennsylvania, William Penn. Through his son, also William, the land came into the hands of the Norris family and in turn to the state who used part of it for a mental institution that opened for patients in 1880. Norristown was regarded as a progressive hospital, as it was the first in the land to employ female doctors. Also, in its early days the hospital "was showing leadership in the field of psychiatry. Straight jackets were never used... moral therapy was advocated."[153] And as early as 1881, Norristown had a bowling alley and a billiards room as leisure facilities for the patients. In 1916, John McDermott's official diagnosis was that he was suffering from chronic schizophrenia but back then, there was little by way of medication, or alternative treatments, to help contain the illness. However, golfing friends began to rally around to support him, starting with the PGA of America.

In January 1916, wealthy businessman and aviator, Rodman Wanamaker, hosted a lunch at the Taplow Club, New York. Among the invited guests were Francis Ouimet, Walter Hagen and A.W. Tillinghast. Their aim was to "form an association of professional golfers of national scope." This was an important step for the pros in getting away from the more amateur-centred governance of golf. Wanamaker also promised to donate prize money and a trophy for a match-play, professional only, tournament. So, out of that meeting came the Professional Golfers Association and the PGA Championship with the first winner in 1916, Jim Barnes, receiving the Wannamaker Trophy plus a check for $500. Six months later and just three days after McDermott was institutionalized, the PGA held its first formal meeting. The first order of business was that "A subscription is taken up for J. McDermott who was reported as permanently sick."[154] One year later, in January 1917, at the PGA annual meeting, the aforementioned Harrison Townsend, the man connected to the Knights of Columbus, of Aronimink, thanked the gathering for a $50 donation to the John McDermott fund.

Separately, the role of the PGA was acknowledged in McDermott's home city of Philadelphia when it as reported that, "Prolonged clapping greeted the announcement last night at the annual meeting of the Golf Association of

152 *Golf Digest*, June, 1977.
153 Norristown State Hospital Archives.
154 Glenn.

Philadelphia that Jack McDermott......was now almost recovered from his illness and that there had been generous responses from local golfers to an appeal for the hospital expenses of the famous player. Golfers at the meeting were particularly delighted with the announcement that a very large sum had been raised for McDermott by the Professional Golfers Association of the United States whose members showed that they had not forgotten Jack, though it had been several years since he has played in their midst."[155]

When The United States entered World War One in April 1917, golf partially paused, in that no U.S. Open, U.S. Amateur, or U.S. Women's Amateur, championships were held that year. The same applied in 1918. However, this did not mean the game itself was suspended. Initially there was some skepticism that playing golf might be seen as out of step with the mood of a nation at war. In fact, golf's popularity soared during this two-year period. This was largely due to the number of exhibition matches held to raise funds for the war effort. The Red Cross, in particular, benefited to a great degree. These exhibitions, extensively reported on by the national newspapers, caught the public's imagination and were widely supported. And, the fund drive was greatly helped by the golf-playing President, Woodrow Wilson, who enthusiastically backed the initiative. Many players such as Chick Evans, Bobby Jones, and the reigning U.S. Women's Amateur champion, Alexa Stirling, took part in these exhibitions.

And the PGA was not found wanting in this regard. For example, at Englewood in July 1917, the Association ran a "Classic" for "The War Relief Fund." Many top pros such as Mike Brady, Tom McNamara, Walter Hagen, and Gil Nicolls were on hand to compete. The importance of the tournament could be gauged by the presence of Grantland Rice, who was on hand to report the proceedings in some detail.[156] Willie MacFarlane, who would claim the U.S. Open title in 1925, won the 36-hole tournament. In all of this, however, John McDermott was unable to contribute to the war effort in any meaningful way. The "occupation" section of his draft card read "Patient," and it was stamped, "State Hospital for the Insane."[157]

However, in the summer of 1917, some rare good news appeared concerning McDermott's health when his friend and benefactor, Harrison Townsend, told the media that he "was pleased to report that McDermott's mental and physical

155 *The Evening Public Ledger*, Jan 18, 1917.
156 *The New York Tribune*, July 26, 1917.
157 Merion G.C. Archives.

condition has improved considerably; so much so that his family and I are seriously considering having him released and trying to complete his care by private treatment, which would require a personal attendant, etc, thereby increasing his care for a limited time."[158] Two things were clear from this statement. First, that Harrison Townsend was now acting as a family spokesman as well as a fund raiser for John McDermott, and second, that despite the help from the PGA and others, more money would be needed to help the golfer's recovery. In this regard, at roughly the same time, another statement, this time in *The Evening Public Ledger,* spelled out clearly what was at stake. In a lengthy article, partly headlined, "Golfers Asked To Assist Former Champion," the piece continued, "The golfers of Philadelphia have been asked to help attain this end and sometime this week will receive a letter from Harrison Townsend..................asking for funds for that purpose." Furthermore, it was noted that "While Jack made big money, it has been gone for several years and the cost of maintenance at Norristown has been defrayed largely by the golfers of Philadelphia."[159]

Again, the question of McDermott and money surfaces here. *The Public Ledger's article* suggests that the big money was gone "several years" ago, yet it was only four years since McDermott was a tournament winner and had been head pro at the Atlantic City Club. In addition, we know that the official cost when he entered Norristown just a year earlier was $1.75 per week. But there was the cost, for a short time, of his stay at the Brae Burn sanitarium. Overall, however, it can only be assumed that the bad investments which McDermott suffered from a few years earlier had taken any capital he had, and that for the previous year or two, he was living on a week- by -week basis. But that so many stepped up to help him during such a dark period in his life was a sign of the esteem in which he was held.

Nonetheless, as well as reports on McDermott's health and lack of funds, there were other newspaper references to his golf and in particular, what he had contributed to the game in America. In the decades which followed, Walter Hagen would rightly be seen as the man who dragged the pros from the caddy shack into the clubhouse. However, in his own way, McDermott also raised the profile of the homebreds and helped them acquire greater respect than was the case previously. After his 1912 victory at Buffalo, it was suggested that prior to McDermott's successes, and in reference to Scottish professionals especially, in order to attain a

158 *The Brooklyn Daily Eagle*, July 23, 1917.
159 *The Evening Public Ledger*, July 13, 1917,

prominent post, a golf club was only considered "the real thing" when it had a pro with "the odor of heather or whins about him."[160] As the newspapers reflected on his career, his contribution to American golf was further recognized. As one report put it, "The meaning of this coming to the front of American golf is something more than the mere honor of capturing the championship each year. It means that the glamor of the British-bred pros has disappeared. Up to the victory of McDermott, it was thought by the big country and golf clubs of The United States that the only proper thing, of course, was to have an imported professional, that without him the club would lack a certain quality of tone."[161] The successive U.S. Open wins of McDermott in 1911 and 1912, had not only ended foreign dominance on the course, it had shown the golfing world that the homebreds were also worthy of consideration when it came to filling the professional's position at America's more prestigious clubs. And while winning big tournaments was of great importance, there was no denying that finding a good club job was the bread and butter on which the pros depended. John McDermott's role in changing how the homebreds were perceived was significant.

Despite his ongoing health issues, in the Fall of 1917, there was a public sighting of John McDermott in more familiar surroundings with a report which again showed the respect in which he was still held by the golfing public. This took place in his home city of Philadelphia when it was reported that, "It must have been a trying order for J.J. McDermott to appear in the role of spectator at the recent Philadelphia open golf championship at Merion. Those who saw the erstwhile great golfer recalled his exploits of only a few years ago and many of those who shook him by the hand expressed the hope that he his recovery would be so complete that another season would find him again competing in open events" The reported also noted that "McDermott looked considerably older than when he was fighting for the chief title."[162] This report was noteworthy on three counts: first, it was encouraging that McDermott had appeared on the golf course again, if only as a spectator; second, there remained a great deal of good will towards him; but third, the fact that he looked much older than when he was winning his titles was disturbing, when we consider he was still only 26. Many top players have hardly reached their peak by this stage and yet here was, a two-time U.S. Open champion, having aged considerably in a few short years.

160 *The Brooklyn Daily Eagle*, August 16, 1912.
161 *The Hartford Courant*, August 12, 1917.
162 *The Sun*, October 7, 1917.

The support and the financial aid did not end in 1917. For example, in October 1922, there was a star-studded benefit match at the famed Merion club, where John McDermott won the Philadelphia Open in 1913. This contest featured Walter Hagen and Joe Kirkwood versus Jim Barnes and Johnny Farrell and was deemed to be of such importance that Perry Lewis, in *The Philadelphia Inquirer*, gave more column inches to his report than was usually the case for a 72-hole professional tournament. And, the journalist gave the benefit match the complete literary treatment including a reference to a great friendship of Greek mythology when nominating Hagen and Kirkwood as the "Damon and Pythias of the links." As for the on-course activities, "From many angles," Lewis began, "yesterday may be regarded as the peak of 1922 golf in Philadelphia, not only because several thousand enthusiastic devotees followed the dazzling play of four of the greatest golf masters the world has ever known, but because the brush which painted the colorful picture at Merion was wielded by the sweet hand of charity. For those four great linksmen were playing, and the devotees were paying in order that Jack McDermott..................might spend the rest of his days in comfort."[163]

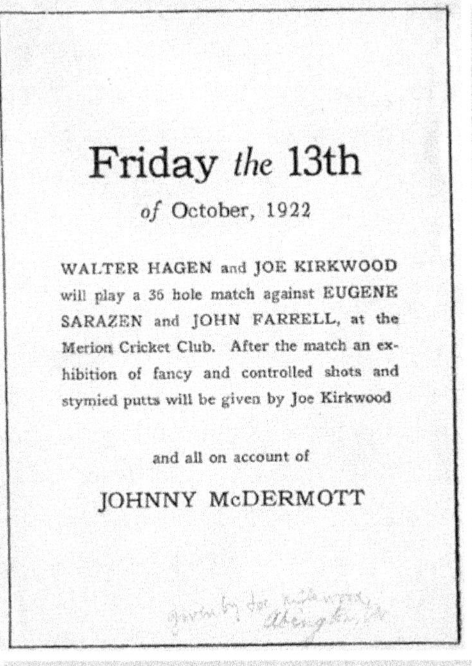

Friday *the* 13th

*of* October, 1922

WALTER HAGEN and JOE KIRKWOOD will play a 36 hole match against EUGENE SARAZEN and JOHN FARRELL, at the Merion Cricket Club. After the match an exhibition of fancy and controlled shots and stymied putts will be given by Joe Kirkwood

and all on account of

JOHNNY McDERMOTT

Notice for exhibition match at Merion. In the event, Jim Barnes played instead of Gene Sarazen (courtesy Merion Golf Club).

163 *The Philadelphia Inquirer*, October 14, 1922.

Although Lewis' report when he claimed the spectators had seen the "greatest golf masters the world has ever known," may have been a little strong, he also reminded his readers that no fees were sought by the players who could have been elsewhere earning substantial fees from exhibition matches. This was especially true of Hagen and Kirkwood who were one of the greatest double-acts the game has ever known who, over the years, would travel the world entertaining galleries: making money; and spreading the golfing gospel. Furthermore, at the time of the Merion exhibition, Hagen was recently crowned Open Champion, a feat that would have only increased his drawing power and remuneration. Their participation was undoubtedly a selfless and generous act by Hagen and the other players. For the record, Hagen and Kirkwood won the 36-hole, better-ball, match, by 4/3 and the Australian treated the crowd to a demonstration of his famed trick-shots to finish off the day. There was no record of what the gate receipts were, but if the crowds were anywhere close to the several thousand referred to in Perry Lewis' report, it should have been a good day for John McDermott.

And, barely two weeks later, the Whitemarsh Valley Country Club held an amateur-professional tournament as a testimonial for John McDermott. It seems that at this stage in golf's history, amateur took precedence over pro as later these events became known as "pro-ams." At Whitemarsh, there were 57 entries and the event was not only a great success but clearly a tournament that was taken seriously. After the 18-hole contest, amateur Marcus Greer and his professional partner, Charley Hoffner, were tied on 72 with Clarence Hackney who was pro at McDermott's old club, Atlantic City, and amateur, Tom Wooton. Greer and Hoffner then won the 18-hole play-off, 75 to 79. These testimonials demonstrate clear recognition, from his peers, for the man who had paved the way for the "homebreds" to take on the invaders. Golfing giants like Hagen never forgot this and he visited McDermott at Norristown from time to time and even played golf on the grounds. Golf courses on sanitarium grounds were not new and were seen as an important part of a patient's rehabilitation. As early as 1894, a nine-hole par-three course was built at the Bloomingdale Asylum in White Plains, New York. Norristown also had its own lay-out, a six-hole course which McDermott possibly helped to construct. On one occasion, when Hagen came to visit, he took McDermott out to play a few holes. McDermott told Hagen, "I don't think I ever saw a more beautiful view than from here. Tell the boys I'm getting along just fine."[164]

164 Glenn.

Gene Sarazen also visited McDermott in the sanitarium, as well as making the case for supporting the former champion. Considering that McDermott had by now received help directly and indirectly from the PGA and from his brother professionals, Sarazen's comments may seem a little strong. However, he was never one to hold back with his opinions, and he was of the view that, "John McDermott,.......has not been receiving that financial aid from his professional brothers that he ought to get."[165] We can recall that at an early meeting of the PGA, in January 1917, a donation of $50 for John McDermott was announced and lauded by the gathering. Now, over seven years later, Sarazen believed that this gesture was not nearly enough. He went on to say, "in the sanitarium where he is staying he has to occupy a general ward, whereas the small sum of $6 weekly would give him a private room." And he continued, "In the case of McDermott, though he has been in need of aid for nearly a decade now, little if anything has been done."[166]

To support his argument, Sarazen cited the fact that PGA tournaments were a great source of revenue and some of this, he suggested, could be used for this deserving cause. And Sarazen went on to explain why he felt McDermott warranted better treatment. "He is especially deserving of unselfish care because he is the first homebred golfer to successfully challenge the supremacy of the foreign bred." And he further opined that "A great many golfers have come into the game since Johnny was at his height, and they have heard a great deal of this little golfer who did so much for Yankee golf."[167] At this stage, in April 1924, Sarazen at the young age of 22, had already won the U.S. Open and two PGA Championships. Like McDermott, Sarazen was of small build and came from the caddy ranks ***and*** from an immigrant background. Perhaps he, more than most, recognized the enormity of McDermott's achievements and how it paved the way for those who followed.

And it was not just with words that Sarazen helped McDermott. In that same month of April, he arranged a benefit match for the former U.S. Open champion which featured himself and McDermott against Johnny Farrell and Morrie Talman. The match was played at Whitemarsh where Talman, McDermott's friend from his caddy days, was head pro. Whitemarsh was an apposite choice as it was near McDermott's care home and he would certainly be comfortable teeing it up with Talman. And Farrell was also a good choice for the exhibition. Like McDermott he

---

165 *The Times Union*, April 22, 1924.
166 *Ibid.*
167 *Ibid.*

too was of Irish heritage and was both a well-liked and respected pro who just four years later, would follow McDermott by winning the U.S. Open. McDermott would also be at ease playing in his company.

Sarazen expressed very clear views on the match and on McDermott's physical and mental state. He said, "He doesn't seem to be in the best of health. He looks under-nourished. At first, he was rather embarrassed and a bit nervous. He didn't play well over the first few holes but I did notice he played everything out regardless of where he was. On the last nine he regained his confidence and then he showed what he was capable of. He played the last six holes in par.......He was undoubtedly greatly enthused about the match and I think if he played regularly he would quickly recover."[168] Sarazen's amateur diagnosis was not far wrong as it was reported that McDermott's physicians had encouraged him to play at Whitemarsh when he could, to build up his physical and mental well-being.

And there were other benefit tournaments for John McDermott that year such as one at the Yonkers, New York, in late July. Many professionals took part and the event was also supported by a number of celebrities, including Al Jolson. The best score of the day belonged to Willie MacFarlane who shot a 71, two better than McDermott's friend, Mike Brady. The following year, 1925, MacFarlane went on to win the U.S. Open. A total of $1362-50 was raised. Then in late August 1924, McDermott himself took part in yet another benefit match- this time at the Langhorne Country Club, in Pennsylvania. Under a banner headline of, "When McDermott Was Open Champion," the local *Trenton Evening Times* gave considerable publicity to a match between McDermott and Whitemarsh pro, Leo Shea, versus George Shea and home professional, John Lamond. It was reported that "a large gathering of Trenton golfers is expected."[169] It seemed that whatever else, 11 years after his last tournament success at the Western Open, John Mc Dermott was not short of well-wishers and supporters. Nor were the newspapers slow to highlight his circumstance and his need for assistance.

Around this time, McDermott also received considerable praise from Charlie Hoffner. Hoffner was also from Philadelphia and had been assistant at Atlantic City when McDermott was professional there. He was also a talented player who, in addition to winning the recent McDermott benefit, amateur-professional

---

168 *The Ogden Standard*, April 27, 1924.
169 *The Trenton Evening Time*, August 24, 1924.

tournament, Hoffner won both the Pennsylvania and Philadelphia championships. He recalled his days at Atlantic City and in particular, John McDermott's dedication. "As his assistant, I used to go to the club early in the morning, but when I arrived, he already would have been there an hour, hard at it." Invariably, McDermott was working on his mashie which was his speciality. Hoffner also recalled a McDermott idiosyncrasy, "He refused ever to use old balls while at practice..............he was afraid that a bit of a cut or a bulge, which would not be in a fresh ball, would cause some deviation from the course he envisioned."[170] This practice would seem a very expensive way of working on your game, even for a U.S. Open champion. However, it also indicates a perfectionist streak in John McDermott and as a reliable and first-hand witness, Hoffner's recollections must be taken at face value.

Apart from these reports, McDermott was also the focus of other newspaper references, mostly in the form of reflections on his triumphs. One of these was an article written by Chick Evans. Evans was a golfer of outstanding pedigree, being the first man to win both the U.S. Open and Amateur titles in the same year- 1916. Like McDermott, he too could be feisty and competitive and it was recorded that there was great animosity between Evans and Bobby Jones. This seemed strange as Jones was one of the most popular and revered athletes in the history of American sport. For all of that, Evans was a highly respected figure and perhaps he saw in McDermott something of a kindred spirit in that both men began the game as caddies and the pair were temperamentally unpredictable. Certainly, Evans' piece on John McDermott was both sympathetic and understanding. Under the heading "McDermott In Sanitorium, Stricken Down By Critics." Evans recalled the following when writing of the 1914 National Open at Midlothian. "I watched him, who should have been better than the best there, receive with a strange look of melancholia on his face, a minor prize...........He seems to have been stricken down with words: they had the power to destroy the future of the simple minded Irish-American lad who was unskilled in the use of them. He had trained himself to be a great golfer. Few men can do more than one thing well in life."[171]

At Midlothian, as we saw, Evans finished in second place just one shot behind Walter Hagen, with McDermott tied for ninth: a minor prize as Evans described it. In many ways, these words are similar to those written by Tillinghast some time earlier in relation to events at Shawnee, and the headline "Stricken Down By Critics" leaves

170 *The Pittsburgh Daily Post*, November 9, 1924.
171 *The Chicago Examiner*, June 15, 1916.

no doubt as to where Evans felt the responsibility lay for McDermott's predicament. Indeed, the view that the young golfer should be judged by his game and not his oratory, was one shared with the famous golf architect and writer. The Press, Evans believed, should have recognized this and acted more generously. And using the words a "strange look of melancholia" is instructive as it conveys not just the impression of sadness but of a man who could not quite fathom where his career had gone. In his comments about McDermott, Evans raised a number of salient points, but most particularly the question of his education or lack of it. This theme was developed in a most insightful way by J.G. Anderson, whom, it will be recalled, had been most supportive of McDermott after his poor showing at Muirfield in 1912.

Writing of a personal travel experience, Anderson wrote how,

> it was my good fortune to return to America on a steamer with a golfer of no mean repute who was also the minister of a large church in Pennsylvania. We got to talking on golf......................and I heard for the first time several things which caused me to regard McDermott as a brighter light than ever before. It will do no harm to remark that Jack McDermott was not a very well educated youth. He had very little schooling............but growing into manhood, McDermott felt his limitations more than most of his friends, or others who knew him but little, to this day realize.

Having set the scene, Anderson went on to describe the minister's experiences with McDermott in some detail. "One day the minister went into McDermott's shop at Atlantic City and engaged McDermott for a round in order that he might take a lesson." The minister then went on to recall how in fact it was McDermott who felt he needed help more than the golf pupil. Quoting directly, the minister recalled McDermott saying, "I never had much education. I should like very much a few lessons both in English and penmanship and if you will teach me, I will be glad to give you golf lessons without charge." In that regard, the minister came round to the Atlantic City Club at 7.30 each morning for an hour's tuition and, "all that summer, McDermott tried faithfully to better himself and succeeded." Anderson then suggested that, "the aggressiveness which he showed on the golf links and in his everyday speech found expression also in his determination to rise above his former environment."[172]

172 *The Sun and New York Press*, April 14, 1916.

The minister also told Anderson that McDermott was so grateful that he gave his tutor a bag and set of clubs as a Christmas gift. Following on from this true account, and the comments of Evans, and earlier from Tillinghast, it is clear that McDermott was very conscious of his inability to speak, or indeed write, in fluent and diplomatic terms. John McDermott was not the first, or indeed the last top golfer, to miss out on a good education, but the lack of it appears to have fed into a certain sense of social inferiority which was very much part of his complex and at times, angry personality. However, it was to his credit, as Anderson suggests, that he was determined, and it seemed succeeded, in improving his education and his social skills.

During the 1930's, Golf in the United States had changed and become even more popular. Much of this popularity was due to the much- loved Bobby Jones and his peerless Grand Slam of 1930. And for the professionals, despite the Great Depression, things were also better as there was now a recognized PGA tour under the auspices of first Bob Harlow and later Fred Corcoran. There was also a greater spread of sponsors, such as luxury hotels in Florida and elsewhere, equipment companies, and local Chambers of Commerce. At most tournaments, for example, there was prize money for the first ten or fifteen places unlike the era of McDermott and others when apart from the U.S Open or the Western, you often had to place inside the first half-dozen to make even small money. In addition, there were further changes such as the introduction of steel shafts which replaced the hickory model of the McDermott-era. And in 1938, a limit of 14 was placed on the number of clubs a player could carry. Up to then, players could and did routinely carry between 20 and 30 clubs with Johnny Revolta and Harry Cooper being prominent in this regard. However, even though John McDermott was something of a forgotten hero at this stage, his name did surface in the newspapers again in the unlikely context of the third Ryder Cup match, between The United States and Great Britain, held at the Scioto Club, Ohio, in 1931.

The article in question highlighted the importance of good golfing relations between "Uncle Sam" and "Jonathan Bull." The article went on to report that "Pro golfers are a personable lot and..........have acquired sufficient poise to be at 'home' on all occasions and acceptable to polished, cultured folk of the world. But there was an occasion when it was sadly different." The premise was to highlight the difference between the more sophisticated social behavior of professional golfers in 1931 and that of John McDermott and events at Shawnee in 1913. Again, the question of education and social skills surfaced. The writer continued, by noting that McDermott was still in a sanitarium and asked the question, "Who would think that an occasion like this present Ryder Cup might have been responsible for it. Well, such is possibly the case."

The writer went on to replay, in detail, what transpired between John McDermott, Harry Vardon and Ted Ray and referred to McDermott's "ill-chosen words." We can recall McDermott's outburst at Shawnee, when in reference to the upcoming U.S. Open at Brookline, he publicly and aggressively challenged Vardon and Ray, with words such as, "you are still not going to take the cup back." And although the writer mistakenly used the word "banquet" as the setting for the Shawnee incident, his report was generally accurate. However, the journalist then went on to provide even more insight into the episode and the personality of John McDermott. "Quite a while after," he wrote, "When the incident had been almost forgotten, a friend of mine was playing with him in a tournament. Several times he heard poor Johnny McDermott mumble and mutter, 'they're after me- the USGA- everybody- they're after me."[173] These comments most likely had their origins in the response from the USGA to his outburst at Shawnee and to the letter of rebuke from the Association's President, Robert Watson.

It is important to recognize that the journalist in question was Ed Hughes, who for many years, was a highly respected writer with the *Brooklyn Daily Eagle*. There is no reason to think that he might invent a story about a "friend" who played with McDermott and who heard him "mutter" about the USGA and others. This story again highlights the schizophrenia and the paranoia that, by this time, were very much part of McDermott's personality. This sense that certain people were after him ever since Shawnee. Perhaps, making a connection between the Ryder Cup and the Shawnee incident is a little far-fetched. One a bi-annual team event and the other an exchange between three professional golfers. However, in terms of perception, what caused such uproar at the time, and for years after, was the damage the incident was seen to have done to U.S/British golfing relations. And, what is not in doubt is the damage Shawnee did to John McDermott, even if some of this was self-inflicted. In this regard, Hughes's analysis is worthy of consideration. Certainly, Hughes's friend "was convinced that an event similar in many respects to the present Ryder Cup matches proved to be the undoing of John McDermott."[174]

173 *The Brooklyn Daily Eagle*, June 26, 1931.
174 *Ibid*.

As McDermott lived his life in comparative seclusion, the golfing world outside occasionally referenced his achievements, usually in the press when U.S. Open time drew near. One such instance occurred prior to the 1935 Championship at Oakmont. Under a banner headline that read, "We Couldn't Call U.S. Open Ours In The Old Days" the article recalled how John McDermott broke the barrier or as the writer put it, he "Crashed The Picture."[175] It began, "Until the confident, swaggering, J.J. McDermott came along in 1911, just 34 years ago, our United States open golf championship was absolutely and completely a possession and plaything of the men who grew up in the golf of the British Isles."[176] Some of the language such as "swaggering" and "plaything" may have been a little extreme, but it was further recognition of McDermott's breakthrough victories of 1911 and 1912 and how since then, it was largely a case of American dominance. This trend continued at Oakmont when one of the championship's surprise winners, Sam Parks Jr, took the title.

Then in 1940, Al Ciuci, did an interview with Ralph Trost entitled "Trail-Blazers." This looked back at the Americans who had led the game to the prominent place it now enjoyed. Ciuici's was an important voice in golf, having started out as a caddie at the Apawamis Club when four-time U.S. Open champion, Willie Anderson, was pro there. In addition, Ciuci had his first outing in the historic U.S. Open at Brookline in 1913. In his interview, Anderson, Jones, and Hagen, et al, were mentioned as "Trail-Blazers" for American golf and when he got to John McDermott, Ciuci's comments were noteworthy. "Johnny McDermott," he said, "wasn't the most popular man in golf. But as a fellow looks back, he can see that Johnny added his bit. He was the confident guy who didn't mind letting you know that you were playing for second place. A little of that false reticence was dropped when Johnny got into golf."[177] As the interview was about those golfers who had led the way in terms of the development of golf in America, Ciuci's remark that "Johnny did his bit" was instructive as it highlighted how the two-time U.S. open Champion had overcome the psychological and golfing barrier that had, up to then, seen immigrant pros dominate the game in the United States. He was definitely a "Trail-Blazer." It was good to see John McDermott's contribution to U.S. golf being remembered almost thirty years after his first National Open victory in 1911.

---

175 *The Pittsburgh Press*, May 12, 1935.

176 *Ibid.*

177 *The Brooklyn Daily Eagle*, April 23, 1940.

And the recognition did not end there. In 1943, ***The Capital Times*** ran a series titled, "Big Shots In Golfdom." This series looked back at Americans who, as young men, made a lasting impact on the game. McDermott was number six in the series, following Jerry Travers and preceding Chick Evans. He was in the best of company as Evans and Travers won both the professional and amateur championships of The United States. The sub-heading for series number six was, "McDermott Was First Boy Wonder," with a further headline of "Put Cockiness In Play Of Pro."[178] In regard to the latter part, he was favorably compared to Walter Hagen in terms of self-belief and the best of American "can do" attitude. It might have added, however, without Hagen's diplomacy.

Little was heard of John McDermott during the War years but from what we know, he remained at Norristown and it seems continued to play golf at the six-hole course on the sanitarium grounds. There had been reports that in the 1930's, he played some golf at the Jefferson Club, Norristown, with resident professional, Bud Lewis.[179] However, in terms of a more formal re-connection with the game, life changed for him when, in 1945, Leo Fraser bought the Atlantic City Club where John McDermott had been professional during his great years. Fraser had an impeccable golfing pedigree. His father, "Jolly Jim Fraser" came to America from Aberdeen and turned pro not long after his arrival. Although he was primarily a club pro, he was also a very good player and in a challenge match in 1920, he and Walter Hagen beat Vardon and Ray at Pottstown, Pennsylvania. A ten-year-old Leo Fraser caddied for his dad that day.

Fraser also caddied for Robert Todd Lincoln, son of The United States 16th President. Leo Fraser would go on to turn professional and in 1969, he became president of the PGA of America. He was steeped in golf history and one of his first acts, after purchasing the Atlantic City Club, was to create a John McDermott room. In time a portrait of the former U.S. Open Champion would adorn the walls. Fraser also told McDermott's sisters, Gertrude and Alice, how much the former U.S. Open champion meant to the club and that they should bring him out for lunch and a few holes, whenever they liked. The sisters were so delighted with this gesture that they gave Leo Fraser McDermott's 1911 U.S. Open gold medal. Fraser kept this on his desk until he died in 1986. Later his family passed on the medal, valued at $40,000, to the USGA Museum at Far Hills New Jersey.

---

178 *The Capital Times*, August 7, 1943.

179 *The Philadelphia Inquirer*, November 8, 2012.

The connection with Atlantic City was undoubtedly a form of rehabilitation for John McDermott and it also kept him in touch with the game. Furthermore, we know that in the years 1956/57, McDermott played golf on a regular basis at the Overbrook Club, just outside Philadelphia. Here he was accompanied by assistant professional, Jerry Pisano. There was a certain symmetry about this as Pisano won the Philadelphia Open on three occasions, the same number as John McDermott. The procedure was that one of McDermott's sisters, who could take him out on day-leave from the sanitarium, would drop him at the club and almost unnoticed, the pair would play. As Pisano recalled, "It was him and me and one caddie and that was it." Pisano then elaborated by further recollecting how he "was always interested in trying to figure out his past, what happened to him over in Europe, but I never got any answers..........It was Yes, No, that was about it." However, McDermott did talk a little when the subject was golf. Pisano again recalled, "He knew his golf. He could talk golf to you- 'I cut that one a little, I turned that one over'." And then Pisano ended his recollections on a rather poignant note. "The scene," he said, "of McDermott walking through the door at Overbrook more than 40 years after his U.S. Open win wouldn't hold a candle to watching Palmer and Nicklaus walk into any golf club to-day. No, because basically, I don't think too many people knew he was there."[180]

Three points are raised by these reminiscences of Jerry Pisano. First, despite all he had been through, John McDermott had not fallen out of love with the game of golf. He was still keen enough to play regularly and it seems clear, from his ability to shape his shots, that some of the old magic remained. Second, however, it was clear McDermott's personality remained damaged by the breakdown he had suffered around 1913 and 1914. Whether or not McDermott's reluctance to talk about the past was due to a loss of memory or the pain of revisiting a traumatic time in his life is open to debate. But it seems clear that whatever the reason, he wished to live in his own world, which was perhaps a peaceful one. And third, the fact that hardly anyone at Overbrook knew that a two-time U.S. Open champion was a regular player at the club in many ways summed up the life of John McDermott from the mid-1920's onwards. He was, almost, a forgotten champion.

Despite his relative anonymity, however, John McDermott continued to attend golf tournaments when these were held in the Philadelphia area. One of these was

---

180 *The Index Journal*, June 14, 2011.

the Philadelphia Classic of August 1966. Here, former President Eisenhower was on hand to present the pro-am prizes and he was happy to meet and shake hands with the former U.S. Open champion. Then, in 1971, the U.S. Open was held at the famed Merion course, a place where McDermott had competed, with distinction, in the past, notably when he won the Philadelphia Open in 1913. On this occasion, the U.S. Open, turned into a battle between Jack Nicklaus and Lee Trevino, with Trevino winning out after an 18-hole play-off. However, a legend has grown around a possible sideshow to the main on-course drama and this took place within the confines of the old Merion clubhouse and its veranda. We know that John McDermott attended the championship and legend has it that he tried to gain admittance to the inner sanctum of the clubhouse but that he was refused as nobody knew who he was. Lore further has it that Arnold Palmer recognized the ex-champion and brought him inside as his special guest. This would not have been surprising as Arnold Palmer had great respect for those, like Walter Hagen, who came before him and enhanced professional golf. If this was the reality, it was a case of one champion recognizing another. A few short months later, John McDermott died in his sleep from cardiorespiratory arrest, aged 79. Both his sisters Gertrude and Alice survived him. He was buried at the Holy Cross Cemetery in Yeadon. His main headstone is simple but there is a smaller one just behind with the inscription- First American Born Golf Champion 1911-1912. It was fitting that the last time he witnessed championship golf, it was at the U.S. Open, held in his home town of Philadelphia.

The very simple headstone at John McDermott's grave (courtesy Merion Golf Club).

# EPILOGUE

In terms of recognition from the world of golf, up to the present date, John McDermott's name is conspicuous by its absence from the lists of inductees into the World Golf Hall of Fame (WGHOF) and the PGA Hall of Fame (PGAHOF). On the face of it this seems surprising as both organizations have honored players who have never won a single major title, never mind two. Indeed, the WGHOF has honored Bob Hope and Bing Crosby, and while both men deserve recognition for promoting the game through their respective tournaments, their presence on the roll of honor, before a two-time National Open champion, seems strange to say the least. Perhaps, McDermott's short career, the Shawnee incident, and his being a patient at Norristown, have counted against him with both bodies.

However, as early as January 1941, and less than a year after the PGAHOF was formed by Fred Corcoran and Tom Walsh, the influential Grantland Rice had his say on the matter. Noting that Ouimet, Jones, Hagen, and Sarazen, would unquestionably be the first four inductees, Rice then named other potential candidates, such as Chick Evans and Jerry Travers, but John McDermott, was first on his list.[181] As it happened, two of McDermott's contemporaries and adversaries, Jim Barnes and Alex Smith, were among those honored by the PGAHOF in 1940. The PGA was quick to start a collection fund for McDermott shortly after its founding in 1916 and this gesture was recognition not only of his plight but also of his contribution to professional golf. On this basis, it seems remarkable that the Association has yet to honor John McDermott.

Regarding the WGHOF, a campaign by the "Friends of McDermott" was launched in 2014 to have him inducted and, unsurprisingly, Arnold Palmer backed the idea with the following words. "As the first American to win the U.S. Open, he was one of the players who changed the face of the Open. He certainly deserves the proper recognition for the victory and his fine career in golf." And, USGA historian, Mike Trostel, added his support with, "Perhaps Walter Hagen summed it up best

181 *The Knoxville Journal*, April 10, 1941.

when he said that Johnny McDermott was the golfer who opened the gates to American homebreds,"[182] This bid was not successful but we know that it can take many, many, years for a golfer to be inducted into the WGHOF or the PGAHOF. Mike Brady, for example, who started his career at roughly the same times as McDermott was inducted into the PGAHOF in 1960. And John McDermott's achievements have certainly been honored by the USGA in the Hall of Champions at its beautiful museum in Far Hills, New Jersey. Along with all other USGA champions, his name and achievements adorn the walls. In addition, the USGA also displays his mashie (five iron) with which he excelled, his 1911 U.S. Open gold medal, and the putter he used when winning the 1912 U.S. Open at Buffalo.

The putter McDermott used and the winner's gold medal he received at Buffalo, 1912 (courtesy Merion Golf Club).

John McDermott was also recognized by the Philadelphia Sports Hall of Fame in 2012 when he became an inductee, and his name stands alongside the many baseball, football and basketball players, who have been honored over the years. The award came 100 years after his second U.S. Open victory. Fittingly, it was accepted on his behalf by Jim Fraser of the family that helped to re-habilitate John McDermott when it bought the Atlantic City Club in 1945. And, in the district where he grew up, on October 9, 2014, a plaque in John McDermott's honor was erected by the State of Pennsylvania, at 1201 South 51st Street, Philadelphia, in front of the Kingessing Library. Besides listing his achievements, part of the plaque's inscription reads, "This is his childhood neighborhood where he caddied and learned to

182 Merion G.C. Archives.

play at the Aronimink Club, once located here." Similarly, in June 2017, a plaque was erected at the Merchantville Club where McDermott spent such a formative period in his professional career. Camden County was behind this initiative and its Freeholder Director, Louis Capelli, Jr, paid the following tribute to McDermott, "It is never too late to honor the achievements of an incredible athlete and American." In addition, Merchantville club president, Mark Fanelli, declared, "We are now officially a historic site."[183] These words and plaques are fitting tributes to the man who truly was a local and national golfing hero.

The plaque erected in McDermott's honor near his home in Pennsylvania (courtesy Merion Golf Club).

In terms of John McDermott's personal life outside of golf, very little is known. This is most likely because his life *was* golf. He never married and, while there was a report of a girlfriend whose parents disapproved of McDermott, there was little else in this regard.[184] We know how important his Catholic faith was to him and this was manifest in his regular attendance at Mass from his early days at the Francis de Sales parish church, up to and including his life at Norristown. And then there was his connections to the Knights of Columbus, a Catholic body, and one which would provide practical help for McDermott after his breakdown. He had friends such as J.G. Anderson and Harrison Townsend and there were also his golfing comrades like

183 www.courierpostonline.com, June 8, 2017.

184 *The Golfers Journal Podcast*, Episode 64.

Walter Hagen and Gene Sarazen. However, perhaps the two most important figures in his life, in particular after he went to Norristown, were his sisters, Gertrude and Alice. Gertrude never married and she and Alice, a widow, lived together at nearby Yeadon, Delaware County. Both were always on hand to maintain his connections to the outside world by way of taking him to Mass or, as we know, to visit golfing friends in the vicinity.

So far, this book has looked mostly at the golfing life of John McDermott, his origins in the game at Aronimink, his many achievements, and the controversies which dogged him. However, the mental health issues which forced his early retirement have also been referenced as it is impossible to look at the life and career of John McDermott without recalling in some detail what was often called his nervous breakdown. And, while it is well beyond the remit of this book to offer a definitive analysis of the nature and causes of his mental health problems, his story would not be complete without commenting on what happened to him, especially within the context of the medical and social mores of his era.

Beginning in 1949, each May the United States has a Mental Health Awareness Month. This is a public acknowledgment that people suffer mental health related issues and rather than try and hide such problems, a public debate is seen as far more likely to be productive in terms of helping those with such conditions. And the program not only looks at raising awareness, it also provides people with tools designed to help them overcome mental health problems. Recent figures show that just over 18% of the population suffer from depression, schizophrenia, and bipolar disorder. The seriousness of the situation was highlighted in 2013 by President Obama when he reached out to the people with the words, "I encourage all Americans to advance this important work by raising awareness about mental health and lending strength to all who need it."

Mental health has also found a voice through sport as in recent years, well-known personalities have come forward to tell their stories. In tennis, for example, the young Japanese star, Naomi Osaka, has been one of the most -high- profile in this regard. She has spoken widely of her "long bouts of depression," and in general, there has been widespread support for what is seen as her courage. And golf has also been at the forefront in terms of raising consciousness with, for example, The Ladies Professional Golfers Association (the LPGA) and The Royal and Ancient (the R&A) both supporting initiatives aimed at helping people deal with mental illnesses.

Individual players have also spoken out. For instance, former Ryder Cup Captain, Thomas Bjorn, and two-time Masters winner, Bubba Watson, have spoken about their own dark episodes with mental health difficulties. And rising star, Matthew Wolff, has also talked about his problems with depression. At the age of 22, Wolff has already taken time away from the Tour to help deal with his issues. Sadly, for John McDermott, even though there was practical help by way of benefit matches, there was no real forum for a proper debate on the subject- a forum which might have enabled him to find help with his problems. Headlines such as "Nervous Breakdown" were about as far as anyone got when it came to highlighting his condition. Raising awareness was a long way into the future.

In terms of defining his condition, from the available evidence, it would appear that John McDermott suffered from schizophrenia. This condition was originally called dementia praecox until in 1907, Swiss psychiatrist, Eugen Bleuler, came up with the term schizophrenia. The word comes from the Greek *schizo* as in split, and *phrene* meaning mind. According to Bleuler, for a schizophrenia diagnosis to be confirmed, several symptomatic elements must come together, such as behavioral attitudes, hallucinations, delusions, and strange ideas. Based on what we know of John McDermott, his behavior, at times, fitted into some or all of these categories. For example, the 1931 article by Ed Hughes of *The Brooklyn Eagle*, recounts McDermott's reaction to the treatment he received after events at Shawnee in 1913. "They're after me- the USGA- everybody," was how Hughes' friend recalled McDermott's words. There certainly is evidence that the USGA sought to make an example of McDermott after the incident with Vardon and Ray, but, arguably, the idea that everybody was out to get him comes under the headings of delusions and strange ideas. And then there was the Shawnee outburst itself. Even though he apologized to Vardon and Ray, the anger and defensiveness in his words are representative of a man with behavioral attitudes. This is not to say that McDermott was treated fairly in the aftermath of Shawnee- he most certainly was not- but the words did not come out of thin air and were probably symptoms of a man with some form of personality disorder.

In terms of how the condition was viewed during the years McDermott most needed help, certainly the newspapers from 1916 to 1920 made little or no reference to schizophrenia. Indeed, in one of the few reports on the condition, a Dr Hall, of Clark University, refers to an outbreak of schizophrenia among Americans who "are likely to get it preserving their neutrality towards warring nations."[185] This reference to divided or split American feelings regarding the Great War was a light-hearted take on a serious condition but very little substance existed in the popular press. And in terms of what treatments were on offer, Electro Convulsive Therapy (ECT) became popular in the late 1930's but without access to his medical records, we don't know whether or not John McDermott received this. Similarly, it is not clear if he received Insulin or Thorazine, which were used at Norristown in the 1940's and 1950's. For a time at least, both drugs were seen as being ground-breaking in terms of dealing with schizophrenia.

What we do know, however, is that John McDermott's condition was non-restrictive and it was not deemed serious enough to prevent him from getting a day pass to go to Mass, to visit with his sisters, or as we have seen, to play a round of golf or attend a tournament. In this regard, he particularly liked to visit clubs in the area, usually on week-ends. For instance, just before McDermott was inducted into the Philadelphia Hall of Fame in 2012, the local *Inquirer* newspaper recalled some of these experiences in a vivid fashion. "On pleasant Sunday afternoons after World War II," Frank Fitzpatrick wrote, "two old women would drive their big car up to the pro shop at Philadelphia Country Club, or St David's, or Merion. From the rear would emerge a tiny elderly man in a dated wool suit even on the hottest summer days and wearing a look that was a bittersweet combination of confusion and re The picture of Alice and Gertrude driving him to a club in the area is descriptive and the words are accurate as John McDermott had long reached a place in his life where at times, he could be forgetful. Typically, these lapses might include his asking to speak with a professional who was no longer at the club. However, when asked about his own famous golfing past, as recalled by Jerry Pisano, he either chose not to speak of it or it was because he had forgotten most of his own glorious deeds. Further outings with his sisters included his catching up with long-time Aronimink professional, Joe Capello, and maybe play a few holes. Recollections from those who knew him during these times were that while he was a man of few words, he was always courteous and polite. This was confirmed by long-time Philadelphia Country Club and Pine Valley member, Francis C. Poore, who played a number of times with McDermott. Poore recalled, "Certainly he was not a conversationalist. But he would greet you with a handshake- those hands were remarkably soft- and he would name the professionals he had seen lately. His comments on the course were seldom

185 *The Washington Post*, July 16, 1916.

other than a compliment, but only if someone hit an outstanding shot. After the game, he would have a soft drink and a sandwich. Then his sisters would drive him back to the hospital"[186] It seems that, regardless of the years in Norristown, John McDermott remained a professional at heart, in the sense that only a pure golf shot would impress him enough to warrant a compliment. And, according to Poore, he also retained his competitive spirit. "We played a match," Poore recalled, "he still knew who was winning and he became extremely competitive if the match was close. Somehow he would manage to gather himself and so many times his best holes were the ninth or the 18th."[187]

This competitiveness, articulated by F.C. Poore, was also recalled by his sister Gertrude in the late 1960's. She told a friend that, "John didn't play much last year and so he's looking forward to this season. You know, I can tell exactly how he plays by the way he acts when he gets into the car for the drive home. If he's quiet I know he was not satisfied. Usually it's his driving; then, if he begins to talk, I know he played well. But almost always he'll tell me he had trouble getting the ball into the hole. I guess once you've been a champion it's hard on you not to play as well as you think you can."[188] Once again it appeared that regardless of his health issues, the competitor still burned somewhere within John McDermott, evidenced by how he was looking forward to "this season," and his concerns over his putting.

Concerning McDermott's day passes, and socializing, this was probably therapeutic for him. As early as 1917, Eugen Bleuler recommended patients be discharged from hospital into a community environment to avoid institutionalization. And we know that around 1919-1920, many of McDermott's friends in the medical profession suggested that he mix and play golf as much as possible to try and find a sense of normalcy in his life. John McDermott never returned to the wider community. However, within the context of asylum living, it appears to have been a relatively benign existence.

Remaining, however, are critical questions that lie not far beneath the story of John McDermott's life - from his early days as a professional golfer, were his sporadic eruptions caused by a mental health issue, such as schizophrenia? Or were these outbursts just because he was a man with anger and maybe even a chip on his shoulder? Witness his confrontation with Alex Smith when he came so close

186 Aronimink GC Archives.
187 *Golf Digest*, June 1997.
188 *Ibid*, March 1968.

to winning the U.S. Open in 1910. Regarding this and other exchanges with Smith, much of his venom was directed at those imported British-born professionals whom McDermott believed thought themselves to be superior to the homebreds. He was certainly driven by the need to prove them wrong.

And there was also the question of his education being the cause of a chip on the shoulder regarding his outlook on life. This was raised by his ally, J.G. Anderson, as being a possible reason for his behavior but it does not stand up to much scrutiny. McDermott's efforts to become more educated were commendable, but, almost without exception, golf professionals from this era came from the caddy yard, with many of their number having to leave school early in order to help with the family budget. However, many of these men developed certain social skills and learned to behave diplomatically. Overall, it would seem fair to suggest, that John McDermott ***did*** suffer from schizophrenia and that it was probably this condition, most of all, that led to his sometimes erratic and at times, anti-social behavior.

For whatever reason, John McDermott was a driven individual and while this may have earned him some unwanted publicity, it undoubtedly helped him as a golfer and ultimately it is within the realm of the game of golf that he should be judged and remembered. In the four years between 1910 and 1913, an era when there were very few organized tournaments, John McDermott won the Philadelphia Open three times- the Shawneee Open- and the Western Open, which at the time was considered a major title. In addition, he finished tied fifth at the Open in 1913, at the time the best ever performance by an American. However, it was the U.S. Open that marked him out as being a special player.

In the years 1910, 1911, 1912, nobody beat his four-round score. He lost in a play-off to Alex Smith in 1910 and won the title the next two years. And the following year at Brookline, he finished just four shots behind, Ouimet, Vardon and Ray. It was an astonishing record on what was (and remains) the toughest examination in American golf. And all of his achievements came before he had reached the age of 23. To attain these heights a golfer must possess many qualities both technical, and of the heart and mind. John McDermott had all of these in abundance. His dedication was legendary (sometimes practicing by lamplight)- his shot-making, notably with the irons, was outstanding- and if he could be over-confident at times, he was also fearless and had strong nerves. As Grantland Rice said, "he was pretty sure to be of his best under the heaviest fire."

And yet, John McDermott has become something of a footnote in the glittering history of American golf. Some of this has to do with his personality, his mental illness, the brevity of his career, and the controversies that followed him. In Google searches for him the word "forgotten" often appears. However, some of his "forgotten" status can also be explained by the presence of Francis Ouimet which I referenced at the start of this book. By all accounts, John McDermott should have been America's first golfing hero. He was the homebred who showed that an American could win the National Open title. And yet, officially, the honor of America's first golfing hero went to Francis Ouimet, and with good reason. He was the caddy who won the U.S. Open and not only that, he beat Vardon and Ray to achieve the prize. In addition, and significantly, Herbert Warren Wind reminded us of Ouimet that, "he was a fine man" .... "He never allowed success to swell his head" ...."He was an instinctive gentleman..........He was the great boy who became a great man"[189] McDermott, was only a boy of 19 when he won the U.S. Open in 1911, but he was seen as cocky, confrontational, and at times arrogant.

When looking further into why it was Ouimet and not McDermott who became America's first golfing hero, it can be argued that certain, snobbish, golfing mores of the day were at play. Even though Francis Ouimet was a caddy, he was then, and he remained, an amateur, unlike McDermott who was seen by many as the caddy boy professional. One status was definitely preferable to the other. However, despite the differences in how both men were portrayed, there was no animosity between the two golfers. We saw how McDermott encouraged Ouimet before the 1913 play-off at Brookline. A golfer driven by jealousy would not act in such a manner. And in his newspaper articles, Francis Ouimet wrote positively about John McDermott, especially when highlighting the importance of self-confidence in championship golf. On one occasion his words were, "Supreme confidence was born in the heart of the unfortunate John McDermott..............He felt there was nothing impossible, within reason, for him." And in a heartfelt tribute, Ouimet went on to say, "I doubt if golfers in general really appreciate the wonderful golfing ability of this same John McDermott."[190]

However, while his fellow competitors recognized John McDermott's contribution to the game, the media and the golfing establishment, preferred their heroes to be quieter and to act in a more unassuming way. In this regard,

189 Wind, p. 85.
190 *The Philadelphia Inquirer*, January 21, 1917.

the evidence presented here suggests that John McDermott was not treated well either by the media or by the golfing authorities. Certainly, there was much praise for the "homebred caddy boy" who won successive U.S. Opens. And it suited the media to stir up the American-British golfing rivalry, especially when a native-born man was coming out on top. However, his supreme confidence angered many and after Shawnee, there was a great deal of ammunition on hand to direct at John McDermott. Some of what happened was his own doing, but that it became a trans-Atlantic, diplomatic issue, owed much to the true feelings and snobbery from sections of the press and the golfing hierarchy.

As a final word, perhaps it was John McDermott's bad fortune to have his great years just prior to the momentous events at Brookline, 1913. However, his golfing legacy is there for all to see, especially his victories in the U.S. Open Championship. By winning the title, twice, he paved the way for all the other homebreds who followed him, such as Hagen and Sarazen. We must remember that before McDermott's victories, no homebred had won the U.S. Open. After his second win in 1912, native-born Americans won the following five titles. Neither Hagen or Sarazen ever forgot John McDermott's contribution to the game and in many ways, this remains a fitting epitaph to a true golfing hero.

# Appendix 1

## John McDermott Career Highlights

**Tournament wins**

- 1910 Philadelphia Open Championship
- 1911 **U.S. Open**, Philadelphia Open Championship
- 1912 **U.S. Open**
- 1913 Philadelphia Open Championship, Shawnee Open, Western Open *

**Major Championship Results**

Year 1909 **U.S. Open**. Finished in 49th place on 322- George Sargent won with 300

Year 1910 **U.S. Open**. Tied with MacDonald Smith and Alex Smith on 298. Alex Smith won playoff with 71—McDermott 75- MacDonald Smith 77

Year 1911 **U.S. Open**. Tied with Mike Brady and George Simpson on 307- won playoff with 80 from Brady on 82 and Simpson on 85

Year 1912 **U.S. Open**. Won with 294 by two shots from Tom McNamara. **The Open Championship** DNQ

Year 1913 **U.S. Open**. Eighth place on 308- four behind, Ouimet Vardon and Ray. **The Open Championship**, Tied 5th on 315- 11 behind J. H. Taylor

*The Western Open was regarded by many as a "major" but because it has never been acknowledged as such, it is not highlighted like the U.S. Open and the Open Championship

**Team Appearances**

- 1913- France Versus USA

# Appendix 2

## The Passing of a Champion

This article appeared in *The Golf Journal*, August 1971, not long after John McDermott's death

**THE PASSING OF A CHAMPION**

Among the spectators at the Open Championship at Merion were the two oldest living winners -Fred McLeod, who won in 1908, and Johnny McDermott, the Champion in 1911 and 1912. It was provident that Merion was the Open site, for it is in Ardmore, Pa., a suburb of Philadelphia, and McDermott lived in Yeadon, Pa., not too far away. He had been unable to travel far for many years and, consequently, he saw the Open only when it was within comfortable driving distance of home. The 1971 Open was to be his last. Not long after the Championship, John McDermott died at his home, quietly in his sleep. He would have been 80 on August 12. With him passed an era of American golf, for John was a pioneer. He was the youngest of all Open Champions, and the first native son to win. With his victory the hold of foreigners over our Open Championship was ended. They would win occasionally, but the native Americans would dominate.

McDermott grew up in Philadelphia and learned the game in the caddie yards around the city. He played in the 1909 Open and finished well out of contention. Then in 1910 the Open was played at the Philadelphia Cricket Club and 18-year.old John tied with Alex and Macdonald Smith. Alex Smith won in a playoff. The next year John again was involved in a tie with Mike Brady and George Simpson at the Chicago Golf Club in Wheaton, ill. This time he won. He was 19 years, 10 months and 14 days of age when he became Champion. He won again the next year at the Country Club of Buffalo, N.Y. This was the peak of his career. Shortly after that he was plagued by a -series of misfortunes-a stock market failure for one, and an unfortunate statement about Harry Vardon and Ted Ray, the Englishmen, after Johnny had beaten them in a tournament at Shawnee-On-Delaware in 1913. McDermott was reprimanded for his remarks, and he was hurt by it. He finished four strokes behind Vardon, Ray and young Francis Ouimet in the 1913 Open at The Country Club, and just before that most famous of all Open playoffs, McDermott cautioned young Francis to play the course and not become overly concerned with Ray and Vardon. When Ouimet won he gave credit to McDermott for helping him with his advice.

Misfortune continued to plague McDermott the next year. He was to play in the British Open, but missed a ferry boat that left early. Some officials of the Championship were understanding and said they would make arrangements for John to play later in the day. McDermott refused special treatment. Then on his way back to the United States his ship, the Kaiser Wilhelm II, collided with a British cargo vessel and sank. Something happened inside John after that. He blacked out as he entered his golf shop later in 1914, and since then be bad been in and out of rest homes undergoing a series of treatments. He played golf occasionally, and whenever be could be would attend tournaments in the Philadelphia area. The players there knew him and respected him, and John would pick a grouping and follow it around the whole course. While his mind may not have been able to grasp some things, he was an acute observer of player styles. Once after be bad returned from a swing around the course, he was asked what he thought of the two golfers be bad watched. "That one," he said, nodding, "is a fine putter. The other one ought to be a truck driver." We've lost a number of old Open Champions within a few years now-Ouimet, Walter Hagen, Jim Barnes, Tommy Armour, Lawson Little, Craig Wood-and now John McDermott. What a legacy they left us.

# Biographical Notes on Players

**Jim Barnes** (April 8, 1886- May 24, 1966)

Long Jim Barnes, (because of his 6ft 4in height) was one of the many British professionals who came to the United States to seek a better life in the world of golf. Originally from Cornwall on the south-east coast of England, Barnes emigrated in 1906. However, unlike many other British-born pros, Barnes never became an American citizen. He was club professional at many clubs such as Broadmoor in Colorado. However, it was as a tournament player that he is best remembered. In total, he won 27 PGA titles including three Western Opens and was twice victorious in the prestigious North and South at Pinehurst. But it was his career in the majors that separated him from many of the other pros in this era. He won the PGA Championship twice, (including the inaugural event of 1916) and he also won the Open once and one U.S Open title. It was perhaps this victory, in the U.S. Open, that was his finest achievement as here, he finished none shots clear of Walter Hagen. Sadly, for him, The Masters did not begin until 1934, otherwise he might have won the professional Grand Slam. He was one of the first inductees into the PGA Hall of Fame (PGAHOF), in 1940, and in 1989, he received similar recognition from the World Golf Hall of Fame (WGHOF). He died in New Jersey at the age of 80.

**Mike Brady** (April 15, 1887- December 3, 1972)

Mike "King" Brady, came from Brighton, Massachusetts, and like many of his era, came to the game through caddying. Because of their Irish heritage, Brady was often linked with John McDermott and Tom McNamara and indeed, the three played many exhibitions together. In tournament golf, Brady had 11 victories but is, perhaps, best remembered for his near misses in the U.S. Open. In 1911, he lost out in a play-off to McDermott and in 1919, suffered a similar fate in a play-off with Walter Hagen. One of his tournament victories came in the Western Open at Oakland Hills, where he also served as professional for a time. He was recognized a being a superb iron player. During World War 1, he served in the Navy and played in many fund- raising exhibitions to help the cause. A young Bobby Jones also took part in some of these matches. Brady was inducted into the PGAHOF in 1960.He died in Dunedin, Florida, aged 85.

**Walter Hagen** (December 21, 1892- October 6, 1969)
Walter Hagen came from Rochester, New York, where he learned the game as a caddie. He took part in the famous 1913, U.S. Open at Brookline where he competed admirably and finished only three shots out of a play-off. However, he then returned the following year to claim the title at Midlothian. He would win the U.S. Open again in 1919 at Brae Burn. However, perhaps his greatest achievements in the majors came in the Open Championship which he won four times, and in the PGA which he won on five occasions. In total he had 45 wins on tour. In addition to these victories, he captained the first six U.S. Ryder Cup teams and played in five of these contests. Despite all of these on-course achievements, many would argue that his greatest contribution to golf was in how he raised the lot of the professional golfer from the caddy yard to the clubhouse and beyond. He dressed and played in a flamboyant manner: he was always good for a quote; and the crowds, all over the world, loved his showmanship. It was no coincidence that in recognition of his contribution to the game, Arnold Palmer was among the pallbearers at this funeral when he died in Michigan aged 76. He was among the first inductees into the PGAHOF in 1940, and he was posthumously inducted into the WGHOF in 1974.

**Tom McNamara (**November 18, 1882- July 21, 1939)
Along with McDermott and Brady, Tom McNamara was the last member of the Irish-American trio which was so prominent in professional golf in the early days of the 20th century. He learned the game by caddying at the Country Club, Brookline, and when he graduated to the pro ranks, he went on to have an outstanding career. Among the titles he claimed were the North and South on two occasions and the Metropolitan and Western Opens. However, like his friend, Mike Brady, he was to experience disappointment in the U.S. Open, where he was runner up on three occasions. The most notable of these was in 1909 when he lost out to England's George Sargent by shooting a final round of 77 to the eventual champion's 71. There were reports that the poor finish was due to his suffering sunstroke on the final afternoon. In the second eighteen, his 69 was the first sub-70 round in the U.S. Open. McNamara, was not especially long, but his deadly short came enabled him to compete with the best of his era. He died, prematurely, at Mt Vernon, New York, at the age of 56.

**Gil (Gilbert) Nicholls** (July 23, 1878- January 17, 1950)

Nicholls hailed from Dover, not too far from the Royal St Georges club on the south-east coast of England. Along with his brother, Ben, he emigrated to the United States. His brother Ben was also a fine player and on Harry Vardon's tour of America in 1900, he was the only one to beat the Englishman- he did so twice. Gil Nichols won a number of prestigious titles including the North and South, the Philadelphia Open and the Metropolitan- each of which he won on two occasions. Nicholls was involved in a serious automobile accident in the summer of 1914 which threatened his career. However, he made a full recovery and the following year, 1915, he won the Metropolitan and Shawnee Opens. Nicholls was also second on two occasions at the U.S. Open. He had many club jobs which were sprinkled as far afield as Delaware and Texas. Nicholls was regarded as a fine teacher and when he stopped touring in the mid-1920's, he spent his remaining years practicing this craft. He settled at the Deepdale Club near Great Neck New York, where he died, aged 71.

**Francis Ouimet** (May 8, 1893- September 2, 1967)

Francis Ouimet, grew up near the Country Club, Brookline, Massachusetts: the course where he caddied and learned the game. His place in American golf was recognized, not only on the sports pages, but on the front pages too, after his historic play-off win over Ray and Vardon, at Brookline in 1913. He was, officially, America's first golfing hero. His playing record was outstanding, as apart from his U.S. open title, he also won two U.S. Amateur titles along with many other amateur championships. And he played on eight Walker Cup teams. He has also been recognized as the embodiment of all that is good in the game as evidenced by his being the first winner of the Bob Jones award for sportsmanship, and on his becoming the first American Captain of the Royal and Ancient. In terms of his playing style, Ouimet was the first top player to popularize the interlocking grip, as opposed to the Vardon model which the great British professional promoted in the early days of the 20th century. The grip was later used by Sarazen, Nicklaus, Woods and McIlroy, along with many other top golfers. Francis Ouimet remained an amateur all his life and became a successful financial advisor. In 1974, Ouimet was one of the first inductees into the WGHOF. He died in Newton, Massachusetts, at age 74.

**Ted Ray** (April 6, 1877- August 26, 1943)

Like his friend and rival Harry Vardon, Ted Ray hailed from Jersey. Of his era, he was one of the most distinctive golfers as he invariably played with a pipe in his mouth and he was a ferociously long hitter. He won the Open in 1912, and he had nine other top ten finishes in the Championship. Perhaps he is best remembered for his part in the 1913 U.S. Open at Brookline where he and Vardon were beaten by the relatively unknown Francis Ouimet. However, it is also important to recall that Ted Ray won the U.S. Open in 1920 at the Inverness Club in Toledo, Ohio. Here he took advantage of a faltering Harry Vardon and with a score of 295, he won the title. He was 43, the oldest man to win the title. In an era when professionals made much of their living by playing exhibitions and other challenge matches, Ray had great success in one day 36-hole matches. He was also captain of the British Ryder team in the inaugural contest of 1927. Although he was associated with Ganton Golf Club for a time, he is best remembered for his days as professional at the Oxhey Club, North of London. He died in nearby Watford aged 66.

**Alex Smith** (January 28, 1874- April 21, 1930)
Alex Smith was a member of a famous golfing family from Carnoustie on Scotland's east coast. After he and his family's emigration to the United States, he quickly became one of the leading British-born pros who dominated the American game at that time. His brother, Willie, won the U.S. Open in 1899, and his younger sibling, MacDonald, also won many tournaments. In his years at the top of the game, Smith compiled an impressive record which included, two U.S. Open titles: two Western Opens; and four Metropolitan Championships. In addition, he lost a play-off to Willie Anderson for the 1901 U.S. Open Championship. Smith also held prestigious club posts and at one of these, The Nassau Country Club, Glen Cove, he coached a young Jerry Travers. Travers would later win both the U.S. Open and the U.S. Amateur titles. Smith was inducted into the PGAHOF in 1940. He died in Maryland at the relatively early age of 56.

**MacDonald Smith** (March 8, 1892- August 31, 1949)
MacDonald "Mac" Smith was the younger brother of Alex and Willie and followed in their footsteps to capitalize on the growing popularity of golf in the United States in the late 19$^{th}$ and early 20$^{th}$ centuries. Throughout his playing career he was seen as one of the game's great stylists and he compiled a most impressive resume with 25 tour victories. These included, three wins in the Western Open and four in the Los Angeles Open. The fact that his tournament victories started in 1912 and ended in

1936 is testament to the quality of his swing. However, like one or two more in the history of golf, Mac Smith is often remembered for not winning a major title, as he finished in the top ten 17 times. One of these was his play-off loss to his brother, Alex, in 1910. John McDermott also lost out that day. Most heart breaking, however, of his near misses, was at Prestwick in 1925, where, in front of a partisan Scottish crowd, he shot a last round of 82 and finished three shots behind the winner, Jim Barnes. Smith served as professional at a number of clubs such as the Olympic Club in San Francisco. However, he settled at the famed Oakmont Club in 1934, and remained there until 1946. Smith was inducted into the PGAHOF in 1954. He died in California aged 57.

**John Henry (J.H.) Taylor** (March 19, 1871- February 10, 1963)
J.H. Taylor caddied and learned his golf at Royal North Devon, or Westward Ho, as it is more popularly known. His place in golf's history has long been assured because of his record in the Open and by his being a member of The Great Triumvirate of Vardon, Braid and Taylor. He won the Open Championship five times, the last of which was at Hoylake in 1913. He was also second to Harry Vardon in the U.S. Open of 1900. This came at the Chicago Club and was part of the tour which promoted the Vardon Flyer golf ball. He was also captain of the winning British Ryder Cup team of 1933. And on two occasions, he won the much-coveted British match-play title. In addition to his outstanding playing career, Taylor was an important figure in establishing the British Professional Golfers Association (PGA) in 1901. From 1892, when he laid out the course, until his retirement in 1946, he was attached to the Royal Mid-Surrey Club. As well as Royal Mid-Surrey he designed many courses, in particular Royal Birkdale which he re-routed, with Fred Hawtree, in 1922. These modifications led to the links eventually becoming a fixture on the Open Championship roster. J.H. Taylor was honored by the WGHOF in 1975. He spent his final years in his native Devon where he died aged 91.

**Harry Vardon (**May 9, 1870- March 20, 1937)
Born in Jersey, Harry Vardon became the game's first superstar. He was a great stylist: he popularized the grip which to this day, bears his name; and his record of six Open Championship victories has still not been equalled. In addition, he won the U.S. Open of 1900, not to mention his loss, along with Ted Ray, to Francis Ouimet in the epic play-off at Brookline in 1913. In total he won 48 tournaments and he also played

successfully in many team matches, such as Scotland V England, which were popular in his era. And alongside all of these achievements, he was golf's first global figure with his tours to America in 1900 and 1913, for example, doing much to popularize the game. Many tributes have been paid to him, notably his being among the first inductees into the World Golf Hall of Fame in 1974. And on both sides of the Atlantic the Vardon Trophy is awarded to the player with the best annual scoring average. (In Europe this is now for the Race to Dubai winner) Vardon was also a course designer of repute with many courses benefiting from his expertise. Among these were the majestic links of Royal County Down, which he modified in 1908. Like Taylor, Harry Vardon was honored by the WGHOF, in his case, in 1974. In his later years he suffered from ill health and died in London aged 66.

# Bibliography

## Books

Frost, M. ***The Greatest Game Ever Played***, Great Britain: Time Warner Paperback, 2003.

Lowe, S.R. ***Sir Walter and Mr Jones***, Chelsea MI: Sleeping Bear Press, 2000.

MacRaild, D.M. ***The Great Famine and Beyond***, Dublin: Irish Academic Press, 2000.

Somers, R. ***The U.S. Open Golf's Ultimate Challenge***, Canada: Collier MacMillan Canada Inc, 1987.

Wind, H.W. ***The Story of American Golf***, New York: Alfred A. Knopf, 1975.

## Newspapers

*The Altoona Mirror*

*The Boston Daily Eagle*

*The Boston Enquirer*

*The Boston Evening News*

*The Boston Evening Transcript*

*The Boston Globe*

*The Boston Herald*

*The Boston Sunday Post*

*The Brooklyn Daily Eagle*

*The Buffalo Enquirer*

*The Buffalo Evening News*

*The Capital Times*

*The Chicago Daily News*

*The Chicago Examiner*

*The Chicago Tribune*

*The Cleveland Plain Dealer*

*The Daily Mirror*

*The Daily News*

*The Daily News And Leader*

*The Duluth News Tribune*

*The Evening Bulletin*

*The Evening Public Ledger*

*The Evening Star*

*The Evening World*

*The Glasgow Herald*

*The Harrisburg Telegraph*

*The Hartford Courant*

*The Illustrated Sporting And Dramatic News*

*The Index Journal*

*The Indianapolis Star*

*The Knoxville Journal*

*The London Daily News*

*The Manchester Courier*

*The Morning Post*

*The Montgomery Advertiser*

*The Newark Evening Star*

*The New Brunswick Daily Times*
*The New York Times*
*The New York Tribune*
*The Ogden Standard*
*The Oregonian*
*The Ottawa Citizen*
*The Perth Amboy*
*The Philadelphia Inquirer*
*The Philadelphia Record*
*The Pittsburgh Press*
*The Public Record*
*The Seattle Daily Times*
*The Seattle Times*
*The Sheffield Daily Telegraph*
*The Sketch*
*The Springfield Daily News*
*The Star Green 'Un*
*The Sun*
*The Sun And New York Press*
*The Times Union*
*The Trenton Evening Times*
*The Washington Post*

## Journals and Magazines

*The American Golfer*
*Golf Digest*
*Golf Global Post*
*Golf Illustrated U.K..*
*The Golf 100*
*The Golf Journal*
*The Golfers Magazine*
*The Junior Golfer*

## Miscellaneous

Aronimink G.C. Archives
ESPN
Francis De Sales Archives
The Golfers Journal Podcast
Merion G.C. Archives
Norristown State Hospital Archives
USGA Archives
www.thecourierpostonline.com

# Index

www.ingramcontent.com/pod-product-compliance
Ingram Content Group UK Ltd.
Pitfield, Milton Keynes, MK11 3LW, UK
UKHW022019190726
13853UKWH00005B/2009

9 798409 425470